C000279345

WORTHING
UNDER ATTACK

EYE WITNESS HISTORY OF WORTHING
DURING THE 1930s AND 40s

LOTTERY FUNDED

WORTHING
UNDER ATTACK

EYE WITNESS HISTORY OF WORTHING
DURING THE 1930s AND 40s

CHRIS HARE

Front cover illustration is taken from Long's
painting of bomb damage opposite the Town
Hall, 1940, courtesy Worthing Museum.

West Sussex Heritage Booklet Number 1

First published in the United Kingdom in 2011 by
Guild Care
Methold House,
North Street
Worthing
Sussex BN 1 1 1DU
history@guildcare.org
www.guildcare.org

Registered charity no. 1044658

British Library Cataloguing in Publication Data
A catalogue record for this book is available from the British Library

ISBN: 978-0-9563171-1-7

Design and production: Mike Blacker
Blacker Design
Hillcroft Barn
Coombe Hill Road
East Grinstead
West Sussex RH1 9 4LY
info@blackerdesign.co.uk

Contents

Acknowledgements

I would like to thank all the volunteers on the *All Our Yesterdays* project, who have helped to give form and substance to my ideas for this book. In particular I would like to thank Robin Baker whose research on Worthing in the Second World War has proved invaluable, as has Philip Wood's knowledge of negotiating Ancestry and related websites.

Very special thanks are due to my three proof readers: Paul Deacon, John Goulding, and Sue Parslow, without whom this book would be overloaded with commas, and burdened with incorrect prepositions and conjunctions (the runaway brain went down the track and it blew!) Thanks also to John Goulding for the indexes.

I would like to thank the Heritage Lottery Fund (HLF) for their funding of both *All Our Yesterdays* and Guild Care's *Time for History* project, and in particular, Dr. Christine Garwood and Hannah Vernon. Thanks are due to Bob Phipps and Julia Johnston at Guild Care, and Richard Childs at West Sussex Record Office, who have continued to accept my idosyncracies and whims with good grace and forbearance.

For producing such an attractive and well designed book, thanks go to Blacker Design at East Grinstead, who were ever ready to respond with professionalism and flare to all my ideas and requests regarding format and presentation.

Thanks also to Martin Hayes at Worthing Library and Kate Loubser at Worthing Museum, especially for their help in finding suitable illustrations for this book (acknowledgements for individual illustrations appear in the illustration captions).

1

Introduction

Deciding on a title for a book is never easy, as you need something that accurately conveys the contents of the book, while also being 'snappy' and appealing to the reader. *Worthing Under Attack* seems to sum up those two intentions rather well. In the 1930s, the town was under attack from the twin threats of the Great Depression and political extremism. These threats may not have been as great in Worthing as they were elsewhere, but they were real enough for those at the receiving end. Then, from 1939 until 1945, the town was literally under attack by Hitler's Luftwaffe. Again, the attacks were not as sustained or vicious as seen in other towns, but they were bad enough and caused death and injury. This book concludes with a look at the immediate post-war period, when society seemed united in its determination that neither the scourge of unemployment nor the horror of war should ever be allowed to inflict itself again on the people of Britain.

This book is a culmination of two projects funded by the Heritage Lottery Fund (HLF). The first, the *Time for History* project, was sponsored by Guild Care, and between 2008 and 2009 resulted in over 80 people being interviewed about their lives in Worthing. That project also had access to the Guild Care archives that dated back to the organisation's origin as the Worthing Council of Social Service in 1933. All this information was collated by a team of volunteers and led to the publication of *Through the Hard Times and the Good – an oral and social history of Worthing* in October 2009. The book contained a DVD which included interviews with Worthing residents who could remember the town in the 1930s.

In many ways, this is a second instalment of the first book. It has been possible to include further extracts from the oral history interviews and to explore new themes. It has also been possible to draw on new research material. The *All Our Yesterdays* project is an on-going research project based at West Sussex Record Office. Like *Time for History*, *All Our Yesterdays* draws heavily on oral history sources. There are hundreds of taped interviews stored at West Sussex Record Office, the earliest ones having been recorded by the late Tony Wales in the 1950s with people born in the 1870s and 80s. Most of the interviews stored at the Record Office were recorded after 1970, and constitute a unique record of social change in West Sussex from the late nineteenth century onwards.

All Our Yesterdays is also undertaking the indexing of periodicals and newspapers held at Worthing Library, including the recently discontinued but much read *Worthing Sentinel*. Another publication that research volunteers have been looking at with interest is the *Worthing Journal* that was published between 1932 and 1940. Rather than news stories, the *Journal* contained a number of hard-hitting and satirical columns compiled by writers with nom de plume such as *Looker-on, Stroller-round and Autolycus*. Their clever and inventive writing style really brings the 1930s to life, and good use is made of it in this book.

All documentary sources are listed under 'Notes and References' at the end of each chapter.

All oral history interviewees are cited by their name and date of birth in the body of the text, e.g. [Chris Hare b.1962]. Interviewees quoted in this book are listed in a separate index that follows the general index at the back of this book. Quotes used in the text come directly from the transcripts of the oral history interviews. Few of us speak in carefully punctuated and measured sentences: rather we frequently hesitate and repeat ourselves, as we seek to articulate our thoughts. This is not a sign of being uneducated or having jumbled thoughts, it is something we all do. As far as possible, this 'authentic voice' has been retained in the quoted interview extracts included in this book. Where the meaning of what is being said is not clear, a word or words may have been added in square brackets to make the meaning more explicit. The removal of text due to repetition or deviation is indicated by the use of ellipses.

This book is the first of a series of *West Sussex Heritage Booklets* that will be published locally and funded by HLF. The next in the series will be written by Barrie Keech and will look at health issues in West Sussex over the last 150 years. These future publications will look at historical themes on a county-wide basis, and draw heavily on the archives mentioned above.

For more information about any of these projects or to make any comments and observations about this book please contact me at – chrisharex@yahoo.co.uk or telephone me on 07794 600639.

Chris Hare
Worthing, April 2011

Opposite: The *Worthing Journal* had some arresting front covers, which from the mid-1930s onwards we taken as paid advertising space by Magiclean, a company that liked to blend topicality with its advertising, as seen in this front cover from the early months of the Second World War.

Another Magiclean front cover, from the Christmas 1938 edition. The *Worthing Journal* was delivered to over 12,000 Worthing addresses, and catered for a largely middle-class readership. Despite its popularity, it was unable to survive the strictures of wartime and ceased publication with its July 1940 edition.

we're not asking for the **Moon!**

The front page of a Worthing Council of Social Service (WCSS) annual report encourages its members to keep supporting the Council's charitable aims. Since its formation in 1933, WCSS has gone through several name changes, the most recent, 'Guild Care', being adopted in 1995. The modern organisation concentrates its efforts on providing services for the elderly and their carers. *Reproduced courtesy of Guild Care.*

Chris Hare gives a presentation to a group of Worthing residents, all of whom were interviewed in 2008 as part of the *Time for History* project, sponsored by Guild Care and funded by the Heritage Lottery Fund. *Picture courtesy Malcolm McCluskey, Worthing Herald.*

This meeting was held in February 2011 so that Chris could show the interviewees the war damage photographs kept at Worthing Museum and extracts from the *Worthing Herald* and *Worthing Gazette* for the 1930s and 40s. Many of the memories of those present are included in this book. *Picture courtesy Malcolm McCluskey, Worthing Herald.*

2

The Rev. Padfield and 'God's Sunshine'

The Rev. Ernest Padfield retired to Worthing in 1934, a year after the Worthing Council of Social Service (WCSS) was established in the town. In doing so, he joined a rising tide of retired people who saw Worthing as an ideal location in which to live out their final years. Retired clergy in particular appear to have favoured the town, and in many cases found it necessary to combat, in word and print, what they saw as the irreligious mood of the times. Although, as we shall see, the Rev. Padfield, on one occasion at least, shocked some of his contemporaries by taking what was for them a very liberal stance on the question of sun-bathing on the seashore.

Shortly after arriving in the town, Padfield was co-opted onto the Executive Committee of WCSS and proved a very effective advocate for the new organisation. Despite his active involvement in the

Frolicking bathers such as these upset some of Worthing's clergy in the 1930s, but excited the columnists on the *Worthing Journal. Picture Courtesy Worthing Museum.*

Worthing Free Church Council and the Worthing Boys Club Committee, he was a tireless worker for WCSS, and was credited at a moment of financial crisis for raising donations from the public that were sufficient to keep the fledgling movement solvent. His easy-going manner and sense of humour won over even the sceptics.

If Padfield had a fault, it was his love of corresponding with those who took a different view to himself in the pages of the local newspapers. The fault was not so much in the diversity of this correspondence – there were few subjects on which he did not have an opinion – but in the great length, and some would say, the verbosity of his letters, which local editors seem to have felt obliged to publish in full. The editor of the *Worthing Journal* was forced to reproduce Padfield's letters in smaller point-size to fit them on the page, while Frank Cave, the editor of the *Worthing Herald*, was forced to declare on one occasion: 'This correspondence must now cease.'

Ernest Padfield's opinions on sunbathing marked him out as something of a liberal, although on other matters, such as temperance, he adopted an uncompromising attitude.

Padfield wrote on the evils of drink and the benefits of temperance; he admonished those who preferred to attend the cinema on a Sunday rather than go to Church; and he was always warning his readers that materialistic pleasures could never outweigh the true consolation that was to be found in the Redemption available to all through the sacrifice of Jesus Christ. In all these things he was at one with his brother clergy, but in 1935 an issue arose that sharply divided him from his more austere colleagues – the controversy surrounding the growing popularity of 'sun-bathing'.

It should be remembered that only a generation earlier, Worthing, like many other seaside resorts, still adhered to draconian bye-laws which stipulated that men and women should bathe on separate parts of the seashore and that all bathing must be conducted from bathing machines, pulled up close to the water's edge. There were also rules that governed the attire of bathers to ensure that no 'indecent exposure of the person' occurred. By 1914, many of these restrictions had fallen into disuse, with families setting up tents on the sands and bathing together in the sea, contrary to the bye-laws.

It was not until the 1920s that the idea of 'sun-bathing' came into vogue – the idea that a person would stretch themselves out on the sand to bask in the warmth of the sun's rays, and, in order to derive the maximum benefit, do so with significant areas of naked flesh exposed. Protests against this new fashion started to be heard from the pulpit and appeared as comments in the letters pages of the local press. However, there were those who appeared to take a perverse pleasure in outraging 'Victorian prudery' and by their behaviour or their comments provoke the ire of those who regretted the passing of the old order. Both these tendencies were very evident in the provocative comments of *Looker-on* in the *Worthing Journal*, whose observations not infrequently bordered on the lecherous. In July 1933 he was rejoicing that: 'The bathing costumes were more brilliant and more completely cut away than ever'.[1]

In a later edition of the *Journal*, *Looker-on* was almost salivating, as he recounted what for him was clearly an erotic visit to the beach one summer's day –

....On a recent visit to Angmering-on-Sea I found everybody sun-bathing, and superfluous clothing was conspicuous by its absence. One enthusiast, having left her bathing dress at home, simply removed her outer garments and lay about in a somewhat brazen brassiere and her knickers. And they were white silk ones. It was remarkable how attentive wives were to their husbands in the vicinity, and one old gentleman was heard to be chanting 'O Gladsome Light', possibly because it was Sunday.[2]

Looker-on adds insult to injury as far as many clergy were concerned by his irreverent reference to the Sabbath. The Rev. Harold Mullett, the locum priest at St. Mary's Broadwater, declared that he was horrified by the state of undress, typical amongst the young on local beaches. *Looker-on* refused to take the Rev. Mullett's concerns seriously, making the wry comment that 'there's something fishy here'.

Hoping for a better hearing in the pages of the *Worthing Herald*, the Rev. A.R. Glover took up the cudgels against perceived immorality, allowing his righteous indignation to smoulder from the page –

There is a strong feeling in the public consciousness that the time has come when the scandal of Worthing's open sore, in the ever-increasing shamelessness of the foreshore indecencies should be finally faced and dealt with by the responsible authorities.[3]

He concluded by declaring that the people of Worthing should take heed of Christ's warning to the people of Capernaum that 'It shall be more tolerable for Tyre and Sidon at the Judgement than for you'. Glover was quite literally warning of fire and brimstone being visited on the sun-worshippers of Worthing!

Yet the Rev. Padfield, so traditional in many of his pronouncements, thought it wise on this occasion to temper virtue with pragmatism and even to exhort the benefit for sun-bathing on the beach, especially for those confined for most of their days to the home, office or factory –

'Thousands are dwelling or working under conditions that their Creator never intended any human being to know, and I claim God's sunshine for these people for that brief summer period when they can get it....We shall get no nearer to the renewal of the earth in righteousness by calling things vicious which Scripture principles do not forbid, and which science, reason and commonsense sanction. There are enough real, unquestionable evils to combat as it is. Sunbathing has come to stay in our seaside places until Society's arrangements make it practicable elsewhere. And what better place than the foreshore could be found?'[4]

Padfield did not endorse the views of another correspondent who could not see why people should have to wear anything at all on the beach, observing: 'I assume it as recognised that there are limits beyond which no person of taste would pass, and I would decidedly support the suppression of what psychologists know as 'exhibitionism'.'

In the very modern tussle between 'reaction' and 'progress', Padfield came down on the side of the latter, and in doing so tipped the balance in terms of public opinion in Worthing. Although prosecutions were made against nude bathers, there appears to be no evidence that the Council prosecuted clothed sun-bathers, even those whose costumes were likely to raise the blood pressure of clergymen and newspaper columnists.

Padfield continued to enter into lively debates in the columns of the press, right up until his sudden death in March 1939, aged 67. Many in the town mourned his passing, none more so than the local press, for whom Padfield had provided plentiful copy. The *Worthing Herald* declared that: 'His letters were not those of a fanatic, but were well reasoned and revealed a keen sense of humour'.[5]

Autolycus in the *Worthing Journal* also expressed his sorrow at Padfield's demise –

> It was a shock to me to learn, on the very day that his last letter was published in our columns, of the death of our esteemed correspondent, the Rev. E.J. Padfield. In the true sense he was a gentle man, and had a sense of humour rare in his class. It was a pleasure to debate with him, however much one differed from the views he held so strongly and so sincerely.[6]

Mrs Greenfield and other WCSS pioneers

Martha Catherine Greenfield was one of the founding members of WCSS, and provided it with the considerable benefit of her many years of public service. Mrs Greenfield was elected in 1914 to East Preston Board of Guardians, the body responsible for the management of East Preston Workhouse. So darkly did the name 'East Preston' shadow over the people of the district, that when, in the inter-wars years, middle-class housing was built in the parish, estate agents invented the name of 'Angmering-on-Sea', so that prospective purchasers would not have to suffer the embarrassment of an East Preston postal address.

The workhouse system for all its horrors was not the fault of Mrs Greenfield, and like many

Mrs Martha Greenfield was one of the town's first woman councillors and the town's first female Justice of the Peace. She was a stalwart supporter of WCSS, even if she could not be persuaded of the merits of Nursery Education. *Reproduced courtesy of Johnston Press.*

Guardians appointed in these years, she worked to mitigate its more inhumane aspects. So well-regarded was she that, in July 1918 with the First World War still raging, members of Worthing Town Council decided to co-opt her as a new member, following the resignation of one of the West Tarring councillors. Due to the war, ordinary elections had been suspended, hence Mrs Greenfield's co-option by a vote of councillors rather than the local electorate. Her opponents in the contest were Mrs S.R.W. Parker, a well-known campaigner for Women's Suffrage, and a Mr G.H. Greenfield (presumably not a relation?), whom she defeated by one vote.[7]

Mrs Greenfield was only the second woman to be elected to Worthing Town Council (as it then was), the first being Ellen Chapman, who had been elected in 1910 and would later find fame as the town's first female mayor, gaining the rare distinction of being re-elected for a second term. Mrs Greenfield did not become mayor of Worthing, but she did serve on the Council for 22 years, becoming one of the longest-serving members and the Council's oldest member, still serving at the time of her death in 1940, aged 77. Moreover, she gained the accolade of being appointed Worthing's first woman magistrate in 1924.[8] She served on the Juvenile Court and on the West Sussex Probation Court.

Following the abolition of the Board of Guardians, Mrs Greenfield became a member of the Public Health Committee and took a particular interest in improvements at Worthing Hospital and the creation of Worthing Clinic, which opened in the 1930s, and still operates in the same building today, between the Town Hall and the Assembly Hall. Not surprisingly she was an enthusiastic supporter of WCSS at its inception in 1933, and became a member of its Executive Committee.

When WCSS took up the cause of Nursery Education, its Honorary Secretary, Mrs Methold, must have had high hopes that Mrs Greenfield, a member of the Borough Education Committee, would play a vital role in persuading the Council to adopt this progressive policy. However, Worthing was not ready for an idea as modern as Nursery Education in 1937; in fact Worthing would not be ready for such an innovation until 1994, when West Sussex County Council finally opened the first nursery classes in the Borough. Mrs Greenfield could not be persuaded of the merits of such a scheme and believed that the case in its favour had been exaggerated,' adding sardonically, 'of course any mother would be glad to have us take her children while she sits at home'.[9] Yet many working-class women, far from sitting at home, were going out to work to supplement the meagre wages of their husbands or even to be the bread-winner. These were the years of the Great Depression. During the winter of 1938/39, unemployment in Worthing reached a record high. Such realities were outside the day-to-day experiences of better-off people.

Mrs Greenfield came from a generation that dedicated itself to public and voluntary service. Whatever her faults or prejudices, there was no doubting her commitment to serving the community, and doing so without financial reward. As well as the activities already described, she was also a prominent member of the National Council of Women, the Townswomen's Guild, and a Freemason. This writer was indeed surprised to learn from Mrs Greenfield's obituary notice that 'she was a member of the Lodge of Progress, No.19, of the Honourable Fraternity of Ancient Masonry', as he had thought Masonry to have been a male-only institution.[10]

Mrs Greenfield died, while still working and still planning her busy schedule. She was in Worthing

Hospital in March 1940, supposedly recovering from a heart attack, but all the time writing letters and completing her diary. She had just written to the Borough Education Committee, apologising for her absence from the next meeting, but hoping for a speedy recovery, so that she could be back to 'torment you all'. However she died suddenly, still sitting up in bed, engaged in her work. Such was the outlook and fortitude of Mrs Greenfield and many like her, without whom WCSS and many other voluntary organisations in the town could not have existed.

Other worthies of the WCSS passed from the scene in the 1930s and 40s. Mr W.S. Simpson, who had trained to be a doctor but gave up the medical life in favour of running market gardens and undertaking voluntary service in the town, died in 1944 at the age of 63. His daughter remembers how an active life was cut short by a condition that these days would be treatable by modern medicine, but for which there was no remedy 70 years ago. It should be remembered that this era, although within living memory, was before drugs such as antibiotics or beta blockers were available to patients. It was still quite common for people to die at an age we would today regard as still quite young.

Geoffrey Jordan was an enthusiastic supporter of WCSS in the 1930s. After the war he joined its Executive Committee and later became chairman.
Picture courtesy of Guild Care.

The Rev. H.T. Wagg was the founder of WCSS' Lancing Section and one of the organisation's younger and pioneering members. He was killed on active service during the war, and as such was the only one of the founder members to die a violent death. WCSS' Annual Report of 1944 records his death as 'a grievous loss'.[11] Another younger member, Geoffrey Jordan, had also enlisted, rising to the rank of Captain. He was reported missing, presumed dead. But there was delight and amusement at WCSS when Mrs Methold received a postcard from a POW camp in Germany. It was from Captain Jordan, apologising that he could not make the 1943 AGM but that he had been unavoidably detained: he hoped that WCSS was 'still going strong'.[12] After the war, Geoffrey Jordan became a prominent member and later chairman of WCSS.

References and Notes

1   *Worthing Journal*, July 1933, p.1

2   *Worthing Journal*, August 1933, p.3

3   *Worthing Herald* Magazine, 6th April 1935, p.2

4   *Worthing Herald* Magazine, 30th March 1935, p.2. The author is grateful to Clare Nitman for her research of this correspondence.

5   *Worthing Herald*, 31st March 1939 (Guild Care newspaper cuttings' file, vol.1).

6   *Worthing Journal*, May 1939, p.5

7   *Worthing Gazette*, 19th July 1918, p.6. The columnist, 'The Trifler' expressed the view that whereas the previous generation may have regarded 'feminine intrusion' in public affairs as being an unwelcome development, the modern mind accepted this 'peaceful penetration' with 'philosophic calm'.

8   *Worthing Gazette*, 27th March 1940, p.5, obituary.

9   *Worthing Gazette*, 22nd December 1937 (Guild Care newspaper cuttings' file, vol.1).

10 Obituary notice, ibid.

11 WCSS, Annual Report 1943/44, p.28

12 *Worthing Herald*, 10th December 1943

3

Battle of the Buses

Competition in the provision of public services appears to have declined during the inter-war years, nowhere more so than in the provision of public transport. Small 'bus operators were forced out of the market by the combined effect of large, monopolistic operators and government regulation. The provision of public services by the state increased during the years of the coalition and Labour governments of 1940 -51. During the inter-wars years, although now largely forgotten, there were political movements that opposed both Capitalist and State monopolies. The best known of these was the Greenshirt movement, but another, which took up the cause in a very literal and practical way, was the Distributists.

Distributism was inspired by the writings of Hilaire Belloc and G.K. Chesterton, who took active steps to oppose 'capitalist monopoly'. One way they attempted to do this was by encouraging private 'bus operators to challenge the monopoly of Lord Ashfield's General Transportation Company in the London of the 1920s. Brightly coloured Distributist buses, with names such as 'Vanguard', 'Mountain Daisy' and 'Silver Bell', took to the streets, taking on the might of Lord Ashfield.[1] Their gallant effort was doomed to failure, as Ashfield used a mixture of price-cutting and appeals to his friends in the government to change the law in his interests. Traffic Commissioners were given the power to decide which operators could run certain routes – and they rarely ruled in favour of the small operator. For a time, though, true competition did exist before monopoly trampled this brief flowering and travellers were left with no choice at all. In Devon, for example, the fight became so fierce that it was claimed passengers' lives were being put at risk as rivals literally attempted to drive each other off the road![2]

In Sussex, the small operators persisted longer than elsewhere, gaining a loyal following for their friendly service and reliability. In Worthing there was Mr Gates' Tramocar service, which operated

Opposite: A Tramocar on Worthing seafront in the 1920s. The early vehicles left the driver open to the elements, although cabs on the later models were enclosed. These small operators were popular with the public, but faced stiff competition from the likes of Southdown, who, some alleged, were able to skew the market due to unfair support from the government's Traffic Commissioners.

mainly in the centre of the town, while in the rural districts, the Silver Queen buses gained a similar reputation. All the time they were being pressured by the Southdown Company, which seemed to have the ear of the Traffic Commissioners. Yet, both these small operators survived until the petrol rationing introduced during the war forced them out of business.

The *Worthing Journal* did all it could to promote the Tramocars (which were only trams in the sense that they were operated by a handle rather than a steering wheel, but were petrol-driven and ran without rails or overhead wires), and to expose what they saw as the failings of the Southdown service. The *Journal* claimed that Southdown buses were too costly, often late and showed little customer care. *Autolycus* even claimed, in an open letter to Southdown, that their drivers' took a perverse delight in frightening their elderly female passengers –

> *I have a complaint that certain Southdown buses make a loud bang when the engine is stopped at the end of the journey. Dear sirs, is this necessary? Cannot your engines be properly adjusted? And is there anything in the suspicion that certain drivers do it on purpose to make the old ladies jump. I hope not.*[3]

But for the Tramocars there was only praise. *Looker-on* described one journey 'piloted by that cherry-faced driver who always wears a smile', and 'that Oxford accent speaking conductor who always has a good word for the dear old ladies he helps in and out'; they were, he adds, 'both good examples of the Tramocar employees'. He concludes his remarks in the same tone of praise: 'I arrive at my destination and clamber out. 'Good-night', says the conductor, 'and, thank-you!' So nice, these tramocar men!'[4]

Not all the conductors, one presumes, had 'Oxford' accents, but the *Journal's* columnists could find no fault in them, even when their announcements to passengers included more than just the stop details, such as one conductor reported as calling out: 'This is Heene Road, sir, where the toffs live'.

Bernard Poland [b.1915] was a conductor on the Tramocars during the 1930s, and may well have been the man quoted by *Looker-on*, for he had a fine sense of humour. His memories of those days in Worthing deserve to be quoted at length. Bernard came from a very poor background and had some rough jobs, including having to haul bodies into coffins for a local undertaker when he was only 14. During the war he saw some terrible sights, including the death of many of his comrades and this haunted

Bernard Poland, who died in 2010 aged 95, was the last surviving Tramocar employee. He remembered the popular little buses with much affection.

him until the end of his life (he died in 2010), but his eyes sparkled with fond memories when he remembered Mr Gates and the Tramocars -

Mr Gates, the owner was from New Zealand, [he] introduced the Tramocars as a convenience for himself and other businessmen. He lived at the Towers [now Dolphin Court]. He had to walk to the Pier, he got fed up with that....

Bernard recalled the generosity of the businessmen who used to catch the tramocar that took them to the station, and their commuter train to London -

The first one used to come out, start from Heene Road, seafront and go round up to the library, pick up all the businessmen. They were wonderful, they'd come to the window [of their homes] and cry, 'I am coming' – we had to wait for them. It was standing room only by the time we got to West Worthing.... They never forgot us at Christmas time ...we used to get £40, £50... every Christmas... we got it New Year as well. They were the passengers – were excellent – they'd give us 10 bob – 'keep the change' when it's Christmas time. But we always looked after them – my goodness – we helped the old ladies out, you know, if they had an umbrella, we'd make certain it was alright, we had, we really looked after the public as a servant, but of course the Southdown didn't like that....

Bernard remembered the battles that Mr Gates had with the Traffic Commissioners in establishing new routes –

....the Southdown tried to run us off the road... it all went through the government in those days... he [Gates] wanted to go as far as George V Avenue, along the seafront and come up through Goring Road and then go to the library – another service – but they wouldn't do it. He tried hard to [persuade] the Traffic Commissioners and eventually they said he could go along Goring Road as far as Sea Lane... 2d any distance.... We'd go to the library and we knew what time the cinema finished and we'd wait there – they'd come out of the Picturedrome, which is now the Connaught, come across and pick us up we'd take them home – nearly always Wallace Avenue, Gerald Road and all that – all the outgoing places. Really good, they had a first class service.

The first Tramocars had cabs which were open to the elements, although, Bernard claimed, 'the drivers never moaned.' –

We had I think ten buses on the go all the time. As we got newer busses, they were improved. The first sort, they never had anything on the side. You can imagine on a rough day, you'd start at 7.20 am – [wind] blowing hard – the driver goes down Heene Road, turn right, right on the seafront.....picked up – you can imagine, the wind and rain able to drive straight through that cab – well cab never had nothing to stop it – he would be wet through before he moved off and he had to stay there until 1 o'clock, but then they relieved us with another pair, you know, but you never got any protection....

After the war, the Tramocars were taken over by Worthing Town Council and were converted into dust carts.

The Silver Queen Buses limped on until January 1945 when they were taken over by Southdown, a moment tinged with regret for the Slindon correspondent of the *West Sussex Gazette* –

It seems strange at present to see the large 'double-deckers' going up the narrow village road to the Newburgh Arms. We all know how efficient the South Down Services are, but many will miss the friendly 'atmosphere' of the Silver Queen, which had the reputation of never leaving anybody behind, and will remember the thoughtful way the drivers had of leaving and collecting parcels at one's door. At times the 'bus may have run a few minutes late, but this may have been because Willie had been instructed to hold up the 'bus while 'mum put on her boots,' – and, naturally, the 'bus driver waited. Mr Walling, the owner of the late company, told me that he started the Service in 1919 with one converted Army ambulance holding 14 passengers; a few years later a 20 seater 'bus was put on, which was the first in the country with pneumatic tyres. Later the service was increased to five. He was pleased to state that Ralph Brown, George Bevis, Roger Poulton, Jack Steadman, and Peggy Farrier have all joined the Southdown Slindon service. Florie Heley has not joined, owning to ill health. Many thanks, Mr Walling, and all your staff for your kind help in the past![5]

Notes and References

1   Wilson, A.N., *Hilaire Belloc* (Penguin Books 1984), p.294

2   See articles and correspondence in *Mid Devon Advertiser* 1922.The conflict between competing 'bus companies was graphically highlighted by a reader's letter from, 'Your Disgusted Correspondent', which appeared in the issue of 20th May 1922, p.10

3   *Worthing Journal*, November 1939, p.6

4   Ibid, p.1 and pp 14 – 16

5   *West Sussex Gazette*, 11th January 1945, p.8

Opposite: Two children tuck into a warming stew at WCSS' Soup Kitchen, set up by Mrs. Methold in January 1939. The winter before the outbreak of war was a hard one, with unemployment rising to record levels. The war cut unemployment at a stroke and new government benefits alleviated much poverty. War, though, was a high price to pay for a fairer society. *Reproduced courtesy Johnston Press.*

4

Hard Times

A whole chapter in *Through the Hard Times and the Good* is devoted to the years of the Great Depression, including many personal reminiscences from people who lived through those difficult days.[1] What follows are contemporary accounts of the 30s as seen through the eyes of the columnists who wrote for the *Worthing Journal*, viz. – *Looker-on*, *Stroller-round* and *Autolycus*. These accounts are augmented from other contemporary sources, including oral histories and local newspaper reports.

As the Depression began to bite, unemployment in Worthing reached a new high with 822 persons registered with the Employment Exchange in January 1932.[2] This figure appears very low indeed for a town with a population of 70,000, but the criteria for registering as unemployed were far more stringent than today: it should also be borne in mind that unemployment carried a heavy stigma, and a man would only register as unemployed when compelled to do so by circumstance. Some men – and it was men who registered – would spend many weeks looking for work before they 'signed on the dole'.

The mid-30s saw an apparent easing of the economic gloom, with a boom in house building, but the apparent improvement did not last, and by the winter of 1938/39, unemployment was rising steadily, reaching a peak in Worthing of 1,193 people in January 1939.[3] It was the outbreak of war in September of that year that transformed the economy, eliminating unemployment and raising – through new state benefits – the living standards of the poor. Conversely, the middle class saw a fall in incomes and property prices. The war proved a great leveller, although the cost was paid in lives lost, both amongst service personnel and on the Home Front as well.

The satirical style of the *Worthing Journal*, aimed at a largely middle-class readership, could appear condescending, even heartless, when commenting on the unemployed or the working-class in general, as the following observations by *Looker-on* from January 1933 might suggest –

This advert from the *Worthing Journal* suggests that while many suffered hardship and loss of income during the Great Depression, others were able to become home-owners for the first time. The year 1935 saw more house building than any other year, before or since.

I was going along Montague Street not so long ago, when I encountered a group of men making the most harrowing and mournful noises upon a strangely assorted collection of barbarous instruments, including banjos and things called phono-fiddles. The great aim of these players appeared to be to strike the note immediately below the correct one, and then slither up to it in a truly agonising fashion. They did this with such gusto that the noise could be heard a quarter of a mile away.... I felt that a bye-law should be passed enforcing silences upon these itinerant cacophonists. One feels very sorry for the unemployed, but 'Auf Wiedersehn' played out of time is not likely to increase one's sympathy.[4]

Looker-on goes on to say that a far better solution to the problem of unemployment would be for the Council to engage such men to 'make up the many new roads in Worthing which are in a disgusting state'.

The same columnist takes up the cause of 'Piccolo Pete', an itinerant musician, who was arrested by the police when he attempted to serenade the Duchess of York (later the Queen Mother), when she visited Gifford House in June 1934. Pete, whose real name was Harry Newland, was fined one pound for obstruction – more than a week's wages for a skilled working man at the time. Failure to pay was likely to lead to imprisonment, causing *Looker-on* to comment: 'It may be that we shall not see his familiar figure, complete with top hat and gaudy apparel, in the town again'.[5]

With regard to the wealthy, the *Journal's* columnists could at times appear sycophantic, whether lauding the opening of the new Portland Club, an exclusive gentlemen's retreat providing 'rooms', entertainment and a well stocked bar; or noting with delight the increasing number of Rolls Royces, Daimlers, and Bentleys cruising along Worthing streets. This, they claimed, was a sure sign that prosperity was returning to the town.[6]

Yet, criticism, even condemnation, of the rich did find its way into the editorial content. In March 1939, as Worthing was coming through a terrible winter which saw WCSS opening a Soup Kitchen to provide meals for the families of the unemployed, *Autolycus* reported that statistics from the Inland Revenue Commissioners showed that, while the poor continued to suffer, the rich continued to get richer.[7] Two months later he appealed directly to the town's wealthiest inhabitants to use their money for the benefit of those less fortunate themselves. Having heaped praise on those people who had donated generously to the Red Cross locally, he asked his readers to –

Think of that other band who have so little imagination that they either waste it or hoard it. Would that I could print a list of those who keep anything up to £20,000 lying idle through sheer ignorance of what better to do with it. I do appeal to them.[8]

Having attended the Goodwood Races in the summer of 1934, *Stroller-round* reported meeting with a Worthing man who had lost £500 in bets in one day. Later he met the man's wife, drowning her sorrows in the bar, who admitted to a similar recklessness. The amusing angle was that both had made him swear him not to tell the other of their losses.[9] Mervyn Cutten [b.1916], remembered Goodwood at this time, and how gangs of boys and youths ran beside the carriages taking the race-goers to their enclosures, shouting out for spare change, and were often rewarded with a few coppers thrown in their direction. It was a stark and very visual representation of the inequity of the time and the resilience of the class system.

Con Ainsworth was very well known in Worthing as an archaeologist and adult educator. Here he is seen addressing campaigners on Cissbury Ring in 1988 protesting against a possible A27 by-pass close by. Few people, including the author (seen mid picture with rucksack) had any idea that Con had played such a pivotal role in the National Unemployed Workers Movement in Worthing in 1939.

Many of the unemployed in Worthing joined the National Unemployed Workers' Movement (NUWM), an organisation that came into conflict with WCSS, as well as the Mayor, Alderman E.A. Brackley in March 1939. The cause of the conflict was a curious one: Arthur Linfield, representing WCSS and the Rotary Club, had arranged for a social centre for the unemployed to be opened at the Methodist Hall in Chapel Road from 10.30am to 12.30pm every week day, where the unemployed could read journals and newspapers, or play games, while being supplied with hot refreshments. The Mayor promised to support the Centre and preside at the official opening.[10]

However, the Worthing branch of the NUWM objected, saying they wanted nothing to do with the proposed Centre. The Secretary, Mr H McCourty claimed that any unemployed man not actively looking for work during the hours the Centre was open would be liable to have his benefits withdrawn. This claim was hotly contest by Arthur Linfield, who accused the NUWM of making politically motivated and 'mischievous' statements.[11]

The situation was exacerbated when some members of the local NUWM seceded, claiming that the local leadership were influenced by Communist principles, and that on one occasion at the close of a social meeting, when all had risen to sing the National Anthem, one committee member had instead sung the 'Red Flag'. It was further alleged that the NUWM leadership had stifled dissent and had refused membership to fascists. The breakaway group was to be known as the Worthing and District Unemployed Organisation, and Mayor Brackley promised to preside at their first meeting. The Mayor also deplored the 'political' nature of the NUWM and agreed to become the President of the new organisation.

The NUWM hit back. Mr C.J. Ainsworth, a member of the NUWM and chairman of the Worthing Trades Council, denounced the splinter group as 'blacklegs', adding, 'far from calling it a split, I should be inclined to call the whole thing a purge'. He then addressed the allegations that had been made -

I challenge any members of this new organisation to say whether at any time attempts were made by the NUWM to suppress expressions of their opinions. Every point put forward by them could have been discussed at the NUWM meetings. By breaking away from the national movement how can you be furthering the interests of the unemployed in any way? The whole of the unemployed's agitation in this country has been brought about by the NUWM.[12]

'Con' Ainsworth was very well-known to the author and to many other Worthing people for the fascinating and inspiring lectures he gave on the archaeology of Worthing. Although he was known to have left-wing views, few people knew of his activism during the 30s and 40s. Ernie Blackman [b.1929] remembers the influence Con's political opinions had on him as a young man –

He ran the electrical shop in Brighton Road, opposite the entrance to Selden Road. My brother worked in the shop. Con Ainsworth got me to join the Communist Party. Both myself and my brother were in the Young Communist League. We were big Stalin fans. I believed everything that came out of the Daily Worker [communist newspaper].... We all had this dream that it [communism] would work, until we learnt better. I think he [Con] saw the light as far as Russia and Stalin were concerned and he became more interested in history and archaeology than politics.

UNEMPLOYED SPLIT LEADS TO NEW ORGANISATION

Trades Council Chairman Attacks "Blacklegs"

" IF sections of a movement break away and conduct things in such a way that they sabotage the work of the movement, they are known as blacklegs," said Mr C. J. Ainsworth (chairman of Worthing Trades Council) at a meeting at the Methodist Hall on Wednesday at which Worthing and District Unemployed Organisation was formed.

Some members of the Worthing National Unemployed Workers' Movement have resigned to start a new organisation.

The reason for the split given by several speakers at the meeting on Wednesday was the " Communistic element of the N.U.W.M."

The local newspapers considered the crisis within the NUWM in 1939 as a major news story. *Reproduced courtesy Johnston Press.*

WORTHING GAZETTE   16/3/39.

SOME OF WORTHING'S UNEMPLOYED who have broken away from the Worthing Branch of the National Unemployed Workers' Movement and formed the Worthing and District Unemployed Organisation. Councillor H. J. T. Brackley is seen presiding at the meeting at which this decision was made.

SPLIT AMONG WORTHING'S UNEMPLOYED

New Organisation Formed

There are now two organisations representing the unemployed in Worthing.

Breaking away from the local branch of the National Unemployed Workers' Movement, a section of that body has formed the Worthing and District Unemployed Organisation, and has asked the Mayor (Alderman E. A. Brackley) to take steps to revive the scheme (promoted by the Worthing Council of Social Service and the Rotary Club) for running a social and recreational centre for the unemployed which was recently abandoned owing to the attitude towards it adopted by the Unemployed Workers' Movement.

MAYOR AND THE RECREATION CENTRE

At Monday's luncheon of the Worthing Rotary Club the Mayor (Alderman E. A. Brackley) said he wished to thank the Club and the Council of Social Service for what they had done in connection with this matter of a place where the unemployed could meet.

Previous to the day on which he was to open it, he had a communication which showed there was some friction, and he had an opportunity to report to the Town Council what he proposed doing—to postpone the opening.

He thought it was not the wish of the Club or of the Council of Social Service or the Town Council to associate themselves with any section of the unemployed. Their object was to endeavour to help the unemployed as a body; and he hoped the Club agreed

The Mayor gave his support to the breakaway group, but was the crisis more about the fear of Communist subversion than helping the unemployed?

A few weeks after the Unemployed Centre rumpus, the NUWM sought to assert its authority as the true representative of Worthing's unemployed by staging a mock funeral on the shingle beach opposite The Steyne. They even erected a mock tombstone, bearing the inscription: 'Here Lies the Body of the Unemployed Man'.[13] The point being that the long-term unemployed had been forgotten and abandoned by those in authority.

Today, few people outside the public sector are members of a union and it is easy to forget the strength of the Trade Union movement in the recent past, which included the unionisation of the unemployed. Yet perhaps the most curious aspect of this pre-war controversy from an historical point of view is that it was apparently common practice for a social gathering of the unemployed to terminate with the singing of the National Anthem!

The writers at the *Worthing Journal* were most impassioned when it came to the policies of Worthing Town Council, dominated for much of this period by the Ratepayers' Defence League, an organisation that did not meet with the approval of the town's satirists. The new Town Hall, built at the height of the economic crisis, involved considerable expenditure from the public purse and incited both rage and contempt from *Looker-on* –

For weeks past my fountain pen, charged with vitriol, has been lying on my desk, waiting for the opportunity to pour abuse on the heads of our city fathers for providing, at colossal cost, a super luxury hotel in which they could discuss in comfort further means to bleed the long-suffering ratepayers.[14]

Autolycus thought that the new suburbs rising out of the fields to the west of the Borough would bring in new people with new ideas to loosen the grip of the dead hand, as he saw it, of the Council over the life of the town –

It is becoming almost a whole-time job to keep in touch with all the new suburbs of the borough, so fast do they spring up. I have lately explored the Goring area, which is slowly moving the centre of gravity of Worthing westward, and was lost both in the new roads and in the admiration of the courage and enterprise evident on all sides.... A thought struck me as I strolled past these up-to-date sunshine and electric houses that are, or will shortly be, inhabited by people who take for granted things which thousands of the older inhabitants have hardly yet heard about: Is it possible that this new town and its new inhabitants with their new ideas can be adequately and truly represented by the Old Council with its pathetic belief in the permanence of the Victorian or the Edwardian technique? The answer, I am afraid, is a decided negative.[15]

This clarion call for modernity saw no tragedy in the loss of green fields and hedgerows, neither did it mourn the passing of an ethos that clung to the ideals of pre-First World War society. Little wonder then that all the *Worthing Journal* columnists were as one in denouncing attempts by the Council to govern the town by the light of old principles. They particularly disliked the numerous business ventures that the Council involved itself with during the 30s, including opening and running an Electricity showroom as well as various theatres in the town. They warned that the Council would never be able to build a new swimming baths, left to its own devices – and so it proved: the project was postponed in 1939, and not revived until 1966, leading to the opening of the Aquarena two years later. The *Worthing Journal* did not believe that the old men of the Council could be trusted with the urgent matter of improving the facilities of the town.

All this was very well for businessmen with plenty of capital behind them, but for small shopkeepers, the 30s were bad years. Married couples, often past their prime, worked day and night to keep open small shops, sometimes catering for specialist tastes. In a warning that could be made just as well in 2011 as 1937, *Autolycus* highlighted the large number of small business ventures that were doomed to fail: 'In spite of all the warnings and of the awful examples, more and more people open more and more little shops, paying the most preposterous rents for the pleasure of working themselves to death'.[16]

An earlier chapter in this book highlighted the philanthropic work of those Worthing people who gave freely of their time in order to promote the good work of the Worthing Council of Social Service (WCSS), which continues to this day as Guild Care; but some people chose to do good works in the 1930s of their own volition, rather than working within existing structures. One such person was Edith Stokes. From her modest home at 67 Kingsland Road, Miss Stokes, a single woman in her sixties, did a great deal to help others less fortunate than herself and galvanised others to follow her example. In 1934 she established The Spare Time League, which by August of that year had recruited 100 Worthing women, each of whom undertook to produce two garments every year for destitute children and adults in the poverty-stricken district of Limehouse in London. 'Before winter comes,' she wrote in a letter to the *Journal*, 'the united efforts of us women of Worthing can do much to alleviate the distress of this congested area, where the result of long unemployment is so keenly felt.'[17]

In 1939 she set up the Lonely Folk Aid Movement with the aim of bringing friendship and consolation to the lonely, the bereaved and the neglected. Once again, she touched the hearts of Worthing people, as she once more explained in a letter to the *Journal*: 'Since starting this movement a few weeks ago, I have discovered quite a number of people who have spare time on their hands and a love for humanity in their hearts, and who wish to co-operate with me in extending to all those who are lonely (whatever their race, class, or creed), the hand of fellowship and goodwill.'[18]

Edith was born in Erith in 1885, the daughter of a well-to-do linen draper. By 1901 she was living with her parents and grandmother in Queen Street, Worthing – apparently in reduced circumstances. Her father died in 1911 and her brother was killed in the Great War. Edith continued to look after her mother at their Kingsland Road home, where the mother died in 1938. Edith died only three years later, in 1941.[19] It would seem that her income was derived from the estate left by her parents, and that she dedicated the later years of her life to the care of the wider community, as well as her ageing mother. Such selflessness is reminiscent of Mrs Effie Methold, the Honorary Secretary of WCSS, whose similar devotion to the public good was undertaken without any thought of personal reward or recognition.

Notes and References

1   Hare, Chris, *Through the Hard Times and the Good* (Guild Care), Chapter 2, pp 23 – 42

2   Ibid. p.25

3   Ibid.

4   *Worthing Journal*, January 1933, pp 4 – 5

5   *Worthing Journal*, July 1933, pp 13 – 14

6   *Worthing Journal*, June 1933, p.8

7   *Worthing Journal*, March 1939, p.38

8   Ibid, March 1939, p.3

9   *Worthing Journal*, September 1934, p.27

10 Guild Care cuttings book vol.1, *Worthing Gazette*, 1st March 1939

11 Ibid, *Worthing Herald*, 10th March 1939

12 Ibid.

13 *Worthing Gazette*, 29th March 1939

14 *Worthing Journal*, June 1933, pp 4 – 5

15 Ibid, June 1935, p.4

16 *Worthing Journal*, October 1937, p.11

17 *Worthing Journal*, September 1934

18 *Worthing Journal*, May 1939, p.14

19 Research by Philip Wood on Ancestry.com

For the Fascists the leader was everything, and Mosley perfectly conformed to the charismatic image that nationalist movements across Europe were seeking to promote. Worthing proved to be one of the British Union of Fascists' most successful branches. *Reproduced courtesy Johnston Press.*

5

The Worthing Fascists

Worthing may not wish to be reminded of the fact, but in the 1930s the town had one of the most active branches of the British Union of Fascists (BUF) in the country. Oswald Mosley was a frequent visitor and addressed public meetings on at least four occasions, often amidst scenes of rowdy disorder. The town had a fascist councillor, Captain Charles Henry Bentinck Budd, who served on both Worthing Town Council and West Sussex County Council. Although elected as an Independent (as were most councillors at the time), he was District Officer for the BUF and a highly visible and vocal proponent of the fascist cause.

Jorian Jenks was a farmer at Angmering and the BUF's national advisor on agriculture. In 1937 he was appointed as the movement's prospective parliamentary candidate for the Worthing and Horsham constituency. The outbreak of war in 1939 caused the postponement of the election, so Jenks never got the chance to put his case to the local electorate. Following Winston Churchill's appointment as Prime Minister in May 1940, over 800 British fascists were interned without trial. Knowing that his arrest was imminent, Mosley named Jenks as temporary leader of the BUF, although this appointment counted for little as Jenks himself was arrested only a few days after Mosley.[1]

A small group of diehard racists viewed the BUF as fair-weather fascists, who were not wholeheartedly committed to the racial policies of Hitler's National Socialists. One man who held this view was Arnold Leese, the leader of the Imperial Fascist League (IFL), who mocked Mosley's movement for being 'kosher fascists' and dubbed them the 'British Jewnion of Fascists'.[2] Leese, like his idol, Hitler, was a vegetarian and teetotaller, and fascinated by pre-Christian religions and mythology. His anti-Semitism resulted from his experiences working as a vet in the Middle East during the Great War. Emanuel Alford, the founder of New Era Health Products, was a supporter of the IFL. Worthing farmer Frederick Edmunds was a local member.

Interestingly, Budd and Jenks, in their early public statements, made no reference to racial policies, indeed their views seem far removed from the fascist stereotype. Budd first made his mark locally by opposing those on Worthing Council who wished to ban 'Red Hot Jazz' from being played in the town's theatres and other public venues. Even the *Worthing Journal* believed that the young people of the town should be encouraged to enjoy 'healthy, simple dances, akin to folk dances, such as the Chestnut Tree, the Lambeth Walk and the Palais glide', rather than 'negroid nastiness'.[3] Captain Budd would have none of it, and was not happy with the appointment of a new Musical Director with a 'loathing for Red Hot Jazz'.[4] Red Hot Jazz was the hip-hop of its day and universally detested by all but the young.

Budd also had a reputation for speaking his mind in a forceful, even aggressive manner, which often included personal insults. He vehemently opposed the introduction of speed limits on the town's roads and loudly supported a group of unemployed ex-servicemen who had been involved in a scuffle with the police. On one occasion he was issued with a writ, and more than once he 'stormed out' of a council meeting when he failed to get his own way or believed his views were not being taken seriously. Such antics prompted the *Stroller-round* to quote Lewis Carroll's verse: 'He only does it to annoy, because he knows it teases'.[5]

In 1932 Budd, who had been elected to the Council two years earlier, joined the New Party. This had been established by Mosley following his resignation from the Labour government in 1931, when the Prime Minister, Ramsay MacDonald, had refused to adopt Mosley's plans for increased public spending to get the unemployed back to work. So Mosley stormed out of the Cabinet and out of the Labour Party of which he had been a rising star. Following a visit

CAPT C.H.B.BUDD
(A MEMBER OF THE NEW PARTY WHO ADVOCATES "HOT BANDS")

to Italy in 1933 and a meeting with Mussolini, he became a fervent convert to fascism, and quickly set about turning his New Party into a Fascist Party – the British Union of Fascists. While many of his erstwhile supporters, such as Michael Foot, were appalled and would have nothing more to do with him, others, like Captain Budd, were elated, seeing fascism as a new 'third way' between capitalism and communism.

Budd, like Mosley, had served in the Great War and been deeply affected by the experience. He had also been severely wounded, receiving a bullet wound to the head, which left one of his arms partly paralysed for the rest of his life. The secret files kept on Budd by the intelligence services hinted that this wound may have affected him psychologically, and offer some explanation for his 'unstable mental state'.[6] It is also significant that Budd's family, although middle class, had once been very affluent, with connections to the aristocracy. It would seem that Budd's father may have squandered much of this inheritance, thereby leading to more resentment and possibly explaining Budd's later obsession with 'international financiers' who robbed honest folk of their savings.[7]

Jorian Jenks was attracted to fascism because of its policy of self-sufficiency – the 'autarky' of the German Nazis. He saw industrialisation and urbanisation as corrosive developments that were alienating people from a natural way of living and their true inheritance – the land. Today the environmental movement tends to date its origin to the publication in 1962 of Rachel Carson's seminal book, *Silent Spring*, yet Green campaigners might be surprised to find many of her ideas were articulated by Jenks as early as 1939, when he published his book, *Spring Comes Again*, which argues for sustainable production, organic farming and small, localised economies. He believed that artificial

from left to right, Pete Lock, Tug Wilson, and Ernie Blackman, lifelong friends, who have many memories of Worthing in the 1930s and 40s. *Reproduced courtesy of Malcolm McCluskey, Worthing Herald.*

fertilisers were causing cancers and killing wildlife and that the international trade in food, far from being a way of providing cheaper products, was a trap, impoverishing producers and depriving consumers of real choice. Unfortunately, he also pointed the finger of blame at 'Jewish financiers' and increasingly, as the 30s progressed, aligned himself with the anti-Jewish policies of Nazi Germany.[8]

In many European countries during the 1930s, the middle class, increasingly frightened by the rise of communism, gave their support to fascist movements. This was certainly true in Spain and Italy, and most evident in Germany, where the middle class, horrified by the rise of the KPD, the German communists, deserted mainstream conservative parties for the Nazis. So it is interesting to see what a publication like the *Worthing Journal*, which was unashamedly targeted at a middle-class readership, had to say about the local fascists. Budd featured in a series of articles published on 'Worthing Personalities' in 1933 -4, which was full of praise for the dynamism of the young councillor (he was 36 at the time). The *Journal* was less impressed with the town's socialists, as shown in the dismissive lines penned by *Looker-on* concerning a Labour Party meeting in the town –

> ... a good lady, who having listened long and carefully to a speech by Mr J.R. Clynes at a recent labour meeting, murmured to her friend, 'Liz, I wonder what it's all about?' If this is indicative of proletarian intelligence, heaven forbid that we should ever have another Labour Government.[9]

Yet, from 1934 onwards, the *Journal* adopted an increasingly hostile attitude towards the BUF declaring as early as January of that year: 'Fascism has come to Worthing, but Worthing has shown, through its accredited representatives that it is not yet ready to submit to a Dictatorship.'[10] Possibly Oswald Mosley's open letter to the people of Worthing, published in the local newspapers in October 1933, in which he told 'Worthing to get ready for Fascism' and asserted that 'Britain cannot afford to drift any longer while other nations are roused and saved'[11] by fascism, was viewed with some alarm by the loquacious wits at the *Worthing Journal*. The very earnestness of the fascists and their supporters seems to have goaded *Stroller-round*, even causing him to rise to the defence of old foes such as Worthing Council –

> *I met a lady friend who is a keen supporter of the [fascist] movement the other day, who said, 'I hear you are thinking of joining the Blackshirts'. I remarked to her 'why?' 'Well', she replied, and I noticed that her lips, once so beautifully rounded, had been reduced to two merciless thin streaks of black lipstick, 'If we can only get complete national legislation – that is the termination of all local councils – 'Desist!' I gasped. The thought of losing our own, dear old council was too much for my sensitive nature.*[12]

Ridicule tends to be the main weapon deployed against the fascists by the *Worthing Journal* in the mid-30s, combined with some licentiousness when the fascists happened to be young women, as seen in these comments by *Looker-on* describing a visit to the town by Mosley's deputy, William Joyce, later notorious as 'Lord Haw-Haw' –

> *... one thing which impressed me greatly at the Fascist 'At Home' was the large number of pretty girls who can be seen in the Blackshirt ranks. They like hearing Mr Joyce, too. 'Isn't he great!' one ravishing female whispered hysterically to her neighbour, and when the friend who accompanied me made a suggestive observation about 'rats' she gave him a glare which Jupiter might have bestowed upon Mars during the god warfares of long ago.*[13]

The implication that much of the female support for the BUF was based primarily on sexual attraction rather than ideological commitment adds a patronising aspect to *Looker-on's* comments. It should be noted that not only was Sir Oswald himself a great womaniser, both

A female fascist, or just a lady with a liking for wearing clothes so reminiscent of the BUF uniform? Women fascists were clearly active in the town, although *Looker-on* appeared to think that this had more to do with the physical allure of the movement's leaders than their politics.
Reproduced courtesy Worthing Museum.

Budd and Jenks had several broken marriages behind them, Budd's last marriage being to his secretary and former mistress, Miss Baker. Whatever values the fascist leaders were seeking to instil into the nation, they could hardly, with conviction, include the institution of marriage on their list.

Teri Noice [b.1920] recalls that her sister worked at a dress shop in Montague Street, next to Woolworths, and that one of her colleagues went out with local Blackshirt Leslie Standing, who was a high profile member of the movement and 'a real fascist'. Teri remembers that 'the other girls said she shouldn't have anything to do with him, but she was in love and didn't listen.' Standing, who was later interned, used to stand on Durrington railway bridge, staring out. 'We wondered what he was doing.' says Teri. Perhaps he was imagining himself addressing a great fascist rally?

In January 1934, a debate was held in Worthing on the merits of fascism, between a 'Young Fascist' surnamed Alfred and a Young Socialist, Roy Nicholls. For many years, Nicholls was one of the mainstays of the Worthing Labour Party, taking on its opponents on both

William Joyce, a.k.a 'Lord Haw-Haw', was a frequent visitor to Worthing in the 1930s, where, it was said, he had an especial following among women fascists. In 1946 Joyce was convicted and hanged for treason. This sketch was drawn by a local artist and signed by Joyce himself, and given as a gift to the artist's daughter. *Reproduced courtesy of Johnston Press.*

the left and the right. Before emigrating to Australia in 1970, Nicholls admitted that he was behind the defacing of BUF posters in the town, altering the headline 'Mosley Speaks' to 'Gasbag Mosley Speaks Tripe'[14] – fairly tame by later standards, but a cause of great annoyance to local fascists at the time. During the controversy surrounding the National Unemployed Workers Movement in Worthing in 1939, Nicholls had six Labour Party members expelled for selling the *Daily Worker*, the newspaper of the Communist Party, on the streets of the town.

The *Journal's* columnists tended to take the line of 'a curse on both your houses' when it came to the merits of the two young debaters. *Looker-on* thought that there had been 'an outpouring of hot air', but observed that 'Blackshirts always thunder – on the principle, apparently that if you say a thing often enough and loudly enough, people will believe it;' while 'the Socialists as a whole were extremely well behaved.'[15]

Stroller-round was not taken with young Nicholls, but also grew weary of his fascist opponent –

Worthing's publicity seeking young socialist reminded me at times of a young rabbit, faced by the discerning eye of a hungry lion, who in the shape of Blackshirt Alfred made a consistent attack upon the noisy loquaciousness of his foe. I am afraid, though that on several occasions Alfred badly burned his cakes, for his Fascist politics deeply annoyed the Socialists present and when eventually he launched forth with the words, 'Whether you like it or not you will have to accept Fascism', I confess I thought there was going to be trouble....[16]

Stroller-round comments on the large number of people of all ages who were attending political meetings at this time. In conclusion, he casts aside his usual light-hearted, gentle mockery, to reflect more soberly on the danger that the heightened political climate represented –

.... As I passed out into the foggy night I noticed a group of Socialists, and Blackshirts, including of course Captain Budd, walking behind me. They all gave me fierce glances as I looked round at them; and as I wended my solitary way home, secretly rejoicing in the fact that I was neither a Russian nor a German journalist, the words of Coleridge in his 'Ancient Mariner', no doubt inspired by the midnight barrenness of Montague Street came to my mind –

Like one who on a lonely road,
Doth walk in fear and dread,
And, having once turned round, walks on,
And turns no more his head;
Because he knows a frightful fiend
Doth close behind him tread.'[17]

Roy Nicholls and his wife Dee photographed in 1970. Nicholls was a stalwart of the Worthing Labour Party, and claimed that one respected Worthing businessman had been a prominent fascist in the pre-war years. It would be interesting to know this man's identity. *Reproduced courtesy Johnston Press.*

Here we get an insight into the reason that *Stroller-round* and many people in Britain at the time felt hostility towards both fascism and communism – its foreignness. Several letters published in the *Journal* explicitly take up this theme. Mrs Bell, the wife of the Bishop of Chichester, went so far as to state that the British character was adverse to 'shocks of Communism and Fascism' but expressed itself in support for charitable giving and community effort, as evidenced by the success of the Worthing Council of Social Service – an expression of the 'personal touch' that was 'almost unknown in other countries.'[18] Whether or not this was actually the case, it did probably reflect a generally held belief at the time.

Much has been written about the confrontations and riots that took place in Worthing as result of the public meetings held in the town by the BUF and addressed by Oswald Mosley (please see 'further reading' for details), and it is not intended to repeat those accounts here. Rather, we shall consider how the public, and particularly the *Worthing Journal*, reacted to the worsening economic and political situation of the later 1930s and the role played in that gathering crisis by the local fascists.

Looker-on did not even attend Mosley's first meeting in Worthing because he objected 'on principle' to paying to attend a political meeting and having 'other people's' political opinions thrust down my throat.'[19] It is rather startling to learn that people in the 1930s were prepared to pay to hear politicians speak – today it would surely be the politicians who would have to do the paying, if they wished for any audience at all. Certainly at the recent (2010) general election, the meetings that did take place appeared to be stage-managed events packed with party supporters, held for the sole purpose of being broadcast on the TV news. Seventy-five years ago, political meetings were fiery occasions, where the speaker had to fend off hostile questioning and continuous heckling.

After one particular serious breach of public order which resulted in running battles in South Street and Warwick Street, Mosley, Joyce and Budd were arrested and charged with public order offences. Although they were acquitted at their subsequent trial, it was clear that their private army of blackshirted street-fighters was not gaining the same level of middle-class and Establishment support as seen in other European countries. Legislation was introduced in 1936 banning the wearing of uniforms for political purposes and the staging of provocative marches by such organisations. Although the legislation was general, it was quite obvious that it was targeted at the BUF. In an attempt to curry more favour with the public and evade some of the detail of the Public Order Act,

The riotous scenes following the Mosley meeting at the Pavilion on 9th October 1934 received widespread media coverage. One local newspaper thought the scenes more reminiscent of 'revolutionary Spain' than an English seaside town. Needless to say, the reporter probably had little experience of either Spain or revolutions! *Reproduced courtesy Johnston Press.*

Mosley renamed his organisation the 'British Union', although this was a totally cosmetic exercise, and by 1939 even the movement's own members were adding 'Fascists' back into the title.

The early retirement of Worthing's Superintendent of Police in 1935 was seen by many, including the *Worthing Journal*, as a consequence of his apparent sympathy for the fascist cause –

> *Good-bye Superintendent Bristow. Some of us will remember you for one thing, some for another. But all of us should remember that you and you alone secured for Worthing the one bit of favourable publicity resulting from the recent Mosley case. We refer to your comment, published throughout the country that 'they were just very nice Worthing people.*[20]

Captain Budd c.1933. His dashing good looks, not unlike those of his leader, disguised a turbulent family background that included financial loss and a brother committed to a lunatic asylum. Budd himself survived a head wound in the First World War that left one arm permanently weakened.

Such ironic sniggering was typical of much of the *Journal's* coverage of the fascists, which suggested that they were not going to pay the BUF the compliment of taking them seriously. This extended to a refusal to use a capital 'F' when referring to the Fascists, and an insistence on describing the BUF's lightning strike symbol as a 'magic circle' and a 'childish device'. When graffiti began to appear across the town with both the symbol and various fascist slogans, the *Journal* went on the attack, claiming that such acts showed the Blackshirts to be no more than juvenile delinquents. Pete Lock [b.1924] and Ernie Blackman [b.1929] and many other older Worthing residents remember this pre-war graffiti, especially the large slogan painted on Ham Bridge advertising the British Union's newspaper, *Action!*

Much of this graffiti was signed with the initials 'P.J.' – surely the earliest example of 'tagging' recorded in the town? Pete Lock and Ernie Blackman remember a local fascist by the name of Ben Johnson – 'B.J.' – but the contemporary accounts are clear that it was 'P.J.' Besides, Ernie remembers that Ben Johnson 'hadn't got the energy to go daubing,' and that he later switched allegiance and became a communist! So 'P.J.' remains unidentified to this day, but his activities over a period of two years or more caused considerable irritation in the town. Whereas the town's newspapers and police demanded that the culprit be brought to book, the *Worthing Journal* mocked 'P.J.', and in June 1938, having lambasted the idiocy of his campaign, noted that in Germany a whole nation was in thrall to 'childish devices', i.e. the swastika: 'without which the Nazis seem unable to march, salute or shout.'[21]

This was too much for 'P.J.', who wrote a furious letter to the editor of the *Journal*, which the editor chose to print, presumably in the belief that the tirade would do much harm to the fascists locally. The rant included the following condemnation and threat: 'Kindly refrain in future from writing your filthy remarks and opinions in the *Worthing Journal*. It is quite time for such feeble minded scrawling to cease. The first step towards improving Worthing would be the extermination of people like you....'[22]

Action! had taken to denouncing the *Worthing Journal* in the same breath as the left-wing columnist 'Cassandra' in the *Daily Mirror*, an indication that the *Journal* may have been undermining support for the fascists in Worthing – hitherto one of their most successful branches. Yet the venom of the 'P.J. letter' was such that A.G. Findlay, the British Union's Director of Public Relations, was forced to disassociate the movement from such remarks, while at the same time calling into doubt whether the author of the letter was anything to do with the fascist movement. Findlay felt it necessary to conclude his statement with the assurance that if evidence was forthcoming to link the writer with the British Union, 'we should be only too glad to take action against him.'[23]

The 'P.J.' graffiti campaign continued into the early years of the war. A woman walking across the snowy downs by Cissbury Ring in February 1940 reported a barn covered 'with fascist nonsense.'[24] Yet, despite his notoriety, P.J. remained undetected.

In March 1937, the British Union held another meeting in the town, again addressed by Mosley, where Jorian Jenks was introduced as the Union's parliamentary candidate. *Autolycus* was unimpressed by Mosley, whom he accused of 'bellowing', and even less impressed by Jenks, although he did not doubt he was 'a very nice fellow', who should be thanked for giving permission for part of his land to be excavated by archaeologists looking for the remains of the Angmering Roman villa.[25]

When Mosley next came to Worthing in November 1938, it was in the wake of the Munich agreement and the 'Kristallnacht' pogrom unleashed by the Nazis on the Jews of Germany and Austria. In his speech, Mosley claimed that he had received just as much persecution in England as the Jews had in Germany. *Autolycus* was not convinced and deployed all his powers of sarcasm to dismiss such an extravagant claim –

> *Mosley tried to make us believe that the treatment which he received in Liverpool, London and even Worthing was as bad. If this is the case, Mosley is indeed a brave man. I did not realise that he had been chased down streets by howling mobs of lunatics, beating him and scourging him as he went; that he had been spat on, trampled on, had all his property confiscated and then been sent to a concentration camp. However, we live and learn.*[26]

Following Britain's declaration of war on Germany on September 3rd 1939, the British Union continued calling for peace with Nazi Germany and claiming that the war was been waged in the interests of Jewish international financiers. Mosley toured the country, addressing public meetings. His erstwhile lieutenant, William Joyce, had already split from Mosley and formed the National Socialist League, which urged Britons not just to oppose war with Germany but to actively support the Nazis. Joyce later went to Germany to work for their propaganda department, broadcasting daily to Britain, a treasonable activity for which he was hanged in 1946.

One man absent from the British Union's 'peace campaign' in 1939/40, was Captain Budd, who had fallen out with the leadership over the role of women, who he believed should have the same rights as men within the movement, something vehemently opposed by Mosley.[27] Having been inactive in the Union since 1937, Budd resigned his membership in 1939 and applied to join his old regiment. In August 1939, just before the outbreak of war, he was appointed Adjutant of the 44th Counties Division of the Royal Engineers, with an office at Queen's Square in Brighton.[28]

Meanwhile Budd's former comrades continued to campaign against the war and planned to hold another big rally at Worthing in February 1940. But Worthing Town Council refused to hire them any public venue for the meeting, forcing the Blackshirts to meet in Bognor instead. *Autolycus*, despite his hostility towards the fascists and his belief that '90% of the ratepayers' would support the Council's decision, still thought that it was a black day for freedom of speech. He was also alarmed at the arrest of enemy aliens, wondering if such blanket detentions could be justified. He reported a conversation between a Mr Cobby – a friend of an internee – and the town's police superintendent –

'He has already been in custody for twenty three days.'

'And he can be for another twenty-three days or years, Mr Cobby', retorted Superintendent Lewis, 'I can do anything I like with them in war time'.

'Gott in Himmler!' cried *Autolycus*, 'has not an alien any habeas as well as corpus?'[29]

Autolycus was alarmed at the sweeping new powers given to ARP wardens, but particularly to the police, saying that they were hunting in couples 'as if Worthing were the Victorian 'Seven Dials'.' He was taken to task by one reader when he stated that the police were 'as thick as flies', and responded, saying, 'I could hardly say they were as thick as thieves, could I?'[30] This was edgy stuff, particularly in time of war.

Wartime censorship and a generally accepted policy of building up morale do not seem to have made much impact on *Autolycus*, who continued to make remarks that must have caused disquiet in

In September 1939 German nationals in Worthing were interned as 'enemy aliens'. Following Mussolini's declaration of war on Britain in June 1940, local Italians were also arrested. *Autolycus*, writing in the *Worthing Journal*, was unhappy that these detentions were open-ended and ran counter to the concept of habeus corpus. *Reproduced courtesy Johnston Press.*

POLICE SWOOP ON ITALIANS AND ARREST NINE

Worthing C.I.D. officers swooped on Worthing's Italian residents yesterday morning. Nine men were arrested and taken to Worthing Police Station, and later were removed to a place of internment.

A demonstration took place outside an Italian cafe early yesterday morning, and several large windows were smashed.

Worthing has a considerable number of Italian residents, apart from a number of Italians who have become naturalised. Some of them have lived in the

Earl Winterton And The

official circles. He asked why the government did not fix the price of commodities to help the consumer.[31] He drew his readers' attention to the rising number of suicides recorded in the town since war was declared,[32] and commented that the town's entertainments were at their lowest ebb for fifty years, 'when the Rhine Band played to us on the Pier.'[33] Autolycus promised that there were 'facts louder' than these, but that he did not 'wish to be remanded for twenty-three years!'

A vigorous correspondence was conducted in the letters page over whether or not England's war with Germany represented a civil war since both peoples came from the same ethnic stock. One man believed this to be ridiculous as shown by the simple observation of hat sizes: 'A British hat will not fit a German head – we are not a square-headed people,' he declaimed.[34] Alongside such frivolities, the *Worthing Journal* also published more thoughtful letters, which may not have been seen by the authorities as encouraging the war effort, such as this correspondence from Mary Stedman of High Salvington –

Is it so important what race we are descended from? I think not, but it is important that we should guard jealously the traditions of our country, of justice and fair dealing. Let us not be too ready to believe every atrocity story against our present enemies, but let us bear in mind the great benefits humanity has received from the members of the German race. We then shall be ready when the time comes to make peace, to help them to perpetuate these good qualities, which of late had no chance to show themselves.[35]

This popular good luck postcard from Worthing, incorporating the Hindu swastika, would have become a rarity following Hitler's rise to power in 1933. Even though Hitler reversed the swastika for the symbol of the Nazi Party, no one would have dreamt of sending this card after Britain's declaration of war on Germany in 1939.
Reproduced courtesy West Sussex County Library Service – www.westsussexpicturespast.org.uk

Such sentiments may seem reasonable to us today, but in the Spring of 1940, as Britain was gearing up for war, they did not chime in with the national mood. Earl Winterton, the MP for Worthing and Horsham, addressing a meeting of children and their parents at the inaugural meeting of Worthing Youth Council, thundered: 'Kill all the Germans you can. Kill every one of them!'[36] Although his remarks were condemned by the vicar of Goring, the Rev. D.H. Pilkington as unchristian, few people were in the mood for anything other than all-out war following the humiliation of Dunkirk and the Battle of Britain that was to follow. Winterton also believed that that the British fascists had 'deliberately provoked anti-Semitism and encouraged disorder by their provocative action.'[37] Their suppression was therefore justified in the national interest.

In June 1940, following the orders of the new Prime Minister, Winston Churchill, police across the country swooped on the addresses of over 800 British fascists and their sympathisers; over 100 of those detained under 'Defence Regulation 18B' came from West Sussex – the greatest number detained for any county. Oswald Mosley, Jorian Jenks and Arnold Leese were obvious targets, but many local activists were also seized. In Worthing those taken included George Chubb, John Francis and Leslie Standing, the latter being the boyfriend of the Worthing dressmaker already referred to,

Earl Winterton, a West Sussex Member of Parliament from 1904 until 1955. From 1918 until 1945 he represented the Worthing and Horsham constituency. In 1904 he was the youngest MP, by 1950 he had become the longest serving and 'Father of the House'. He was opposed to the fascists and their policies and a great supporter of the war on Germany. *Reproduced courtesy of Johnston Press.*

whose colleagues at the dressmaker's shop had tried to persuade her to end her relationship with a fascist. Teri Noice [b.1920], who supplied that recollection, also remembered that there were people in Worthing who supported the Nazis, who were not interned. One was her own landlord, Bert Wilmer: 'When the first German bombers came over in the war, he used to shout 'come on boys!' But when, one day, he saw the bombs falling, he pushed past me to get into the shelter – he was as scared as anything.'

But the internment of local fascists received no comment in the *Worthing Journal*, for in the same month – June 1940 – it ceased publication. There is no evidence to show that it closed for any other reason than a decline in advertising revenue and the scarcity and cost of newsprint. But it may be wondered – and this is only speculation – if its editorial commentary in those early months of the war had not ruffled a few feathers. The June edition (published in May) contained the following observation from *Autolycus*: 'A reader tells me that Masters of Fox Hounds get extra petrol rations. Can anyone say if this is true, and if so, why.'[38] Lord Winterton's greatest passion was fox hunting.

Doris Conley, the British Union's 'Women's Team Leader' in Worthing, was not interned, but was sentenced to six months' imprisonment for sending letters to a corporal in the British Expeditionary Force, encouraging him to desert. She also sent him literature produced by the Home Defence Movement – a front organisation for the fascists – which urged readers to 'stop the war and clean up

Six Months Sentence
On Woman Fascist

Letters to Corporal
Stopped in Post

At Worthing on Friday, Doris Conley, aged 24, of Gratwicke-road, Worthing, described as a "women's team leader" in the British Union of Fascists, was sent to gaol for six months on charges of endeavouring to cause disaffection in a person in H.M. Forces and having possession of documents likely to cause disaffection in a person in H.M. Forces.

She was sentenced to three months' imprisonment on each charge, the terms to run consecutively.

The charges arose as a result of letters addressed to a lance-corporal in the B.E.F. being

Met On Board

Doris Conley was sentenced to six months imprisonment in 1940 for sending subversive literature to a member of the British Expeditionary Force with the intention of inciting disaffection. It was stated that she was a "women's team leader" in the British Union. *Reproduced courtesy of Johnston Press.*

Britain.'[39] Was Doris Conley the same woman that *Stroller-round* had met six years previously with the 'merciless thin streaks of black lipstick'?

Many of the interned Worthing fascists were released after a year or so; others, viewed as a graver threat to national security, were detained for longer periods of time. Surprisingly, Jorian Jenks was released in July 1941, on the grounds of ill health – he suffered from acute asthma. Even the avowed Nazi, Arnold Leese, was released in December 1943, again on health grounds. This left only the most senior fascists, like Mosley, still in detention, or those known to have had direct contacts with the German Nazis. It is curious, therefore, that Captain Budd, who had resigned from the British Union before the outbreak of war, was one of the last detainees to be released.

In May 1941, lawyers acting for Budd successfully applied for a writ of habeas corpus at the King's Bench, claiming that he had been unlawfully detained under the Defence Regulations; they also raised the fact that he had volunteered to join his old regiment, and had been accepted. Furthermore, his Commanding Officer had known of his past membership of the BUF, and no objection had been raised to Budd's appointment by anyone in the military. Budd claimed that, whatever his past political views,

WORTHING HERALD, FRIDAY, JULY 11, 1941.

The Worthing

WORTHING'S LARGEST AND ONLY CE

No. 1107   REGISTERED AT THE G.P.O. AS A NEWSPAPER   FRIDAY, JULY 11, 19

CAPT. BUDD TO CLAIM DAMAGES FROM HOME SECRETARIES

THE "WORTHING HERALD" UNDERSTANDS THAT CAPTAIN CHARLES HENRY BENTINCK BUDD, R.E., FORMER WORTHING TOWN COUNCILLOR, HAS ISSUED A WRIT ON SIR JOHN ANDERSON AND ON MR HERBERT MORRISON, CLAIMING DAMAGES ARISING OUT OF HIS DETENTION FROM JUNE 14, 1940, TO MAY 26 OF THIS YEAR, UNDER DEFENCE REGULATIONS.

It is also learned that Captain Budd's legal advisers are considering the question of an appeal against a King's Bench division court's decision on July 2, when it refused Captain Budd's second application for a writ of habeas corpus.

Captain Budd was a member of Worthing Town Council from November, 1930, until 1935. From January, 1931, until 1935 he was also a member of West Sussex County Council.

Captain Budd was first detained under the Defence Regulations on June 14, 1940, on a Home Office order. At the High Court on May 27 this year, this order was described as "a worthless scrap of paper," Captain Budd was granted a writ of hab-

has corpus and released. Early in June Captain Budd was again detained under the Defence Regulations and he applied in the King's Bench Division for a second writ of habeas corpus.

This application was dismissed on July 2, when Mr Justice Macnaughton agreed with the Lord Chief Justice (Lord Caldecote), Mr Justice Stable dissenting on the grounds that the material before the court was insufficient to enable him to come to a conclusion one way or another as to the existence of a reasonable cause for detention.

Captain C. H. B. Budd
(Photo, Gardiner)

Police Make House-To-House Check Up

Nine summonses for evading the ban on visitors were heard at Worthing Police Court on Wed-

What He

THE Mayor ...ing a jolly g on Wednesday

He wrote to ton, chairma Women's Ga expressing his being unable their meeting address on war which he sai keenly interest

He didn't kr to have been himself!

Mrs Hamilto meeting that been relying Mayor to addre

What Ha Done Wit Frui

Worthing Food and has been wait to open a fruit pre But no one has s "Not a pennyw Hance, chief coa Officer, told the week.

Reason? Mr sure, but gave tw planations. One fruit yield had not as anticipated, ar that the extra sug a pound a week for had the effect of re able fruit for hom "The extra pe with what people h to save is just ab for the purpose. Mr Hance explain

Despite successfully appealing against internment in 1941, Budd was re-arrested after only a week – a decision that was upheld by the courts. Did his determined efforts to gain his release and his avowed intention to fight for his country actually make the authorities more resolved to keep him in prison, as his MI5 files seem to suggest?
Reproduced courtesy Johnston Press.

he was a patriot, ready and willing to fight for his country. The Court found in his favour and Budd was released, presumably returning to his home in Grove Road, Worthing. But his freedom was short-lived; less than two weeks later he was re-arrested. Again he appealed, but this time without success.[40]

Budd's intelligence file indicates that the first court case and its outcome had taken the authorities off guard: 'The Bentinck-Budd case has caused a serious commotion in the Home Office', it stated, 'they are shaken to the core about it.'[41] Clearly, the Home Office feared that the success of Budd's application could lead to courts releasing many more of the detainees. Could it be that the intelligence services and MI5 were determined to punish Budd for the trouble he had caused them and keep him under detention for the longest period of time possible?

Another, less conspiratorial, explanation for Budd's prolonged internment may have been his apparent fixation with the two fascist leaders – Hitler and Mussolini. After the war, files held by the former fascist regime in Italy were examined and found to contain a letter sent by Budd to Mussolini's secretary when he visited Rome in June 1937, in which Budd implored the secretary for a meeting with the Italian leader: 'It is unnecessary for me to say how proud I would be to be able to meet the Duce', he wrote, 'before returning to England, to take up my Fascistic duties.'[42] Budd's file also contains a postcard from his mistress, Miss Baker, sent from Germany in 1938, in which she eulogises Hitler and even clams to have shaken his hand.[43] Did such evidence suggest that Budd was far more dangerous to national security than either he or his lawyers claimed at the time of his detention?

In January 1944, the Duke of Bedford took up the case of those internees, still detained under the Defence Regulations. While acknowledging that in time of war, the government was obliged to introduce 'abnormal measures' to control 'persons of hostile origin', he denounced the conditions under which many of them had been detained, which, he claimed, included being locked in cells for 23 hours a day and others acts of 'brutality and injustice'. He specifically cited the case of Bentinck Budd –

> ....*General Sir Guy Williams, G.O.C. [General Officer Commanding] the Eastern Command, wrote a letter to the Secretary of State for War in favour of Captain Bentinck Budd, who was arrested in June, 1940. This letter was suppressed by the authorities and never reached the Advisory Committee [the body that adjudicated on detentions]. When Captain Budd was before the Advisory Committee he was asked to supply the names of witnesses who would speak in his favour. None of these persons were communicated with....*[44]

It should be noted that the Duke of Bedford, formerly Lord Tavistock, was hardly a neutral observer. He was the leader of the British People's Party, and a one-time associate of William Joyce, with whom he had broken over the latter's extreme anti-Semitism and his avowed intention to fight for Germany rather than Britain in the event of war. Whether because of or despite the Duke's intervention, Budd was released during the summer of 1944, by which time he was said to be in poor health. He applied again to rejoin his old regiment, but was refused.[45]

Budd may have briefly returned to Worthing, as one local resident did meet him after the war and found him 'a changed man'.[46] By 1952 he was living at Wellings Farm near Ashurst. MI5 continued to monitor Budd's movements until 1954, when they finally concluded he was no longer of interest to them – he had been under surveillance for a total of 21 years. After the war he married his mistress,

Enid Baker. She died in Merton, Surrey, in 1996, but there is no record for Budd's death, suggesting he may have died overseas. It is interesting that one of his grandsons married a woman with a Jewish surname, suggesting that the influence of anti-Semitic beliefs was not extended to future generations of the Budd family.

As for Jorian Jenks, although he continued to advise Oswald Mosley on policy matters after the war, he did not join Mosley's new Union Movement. Jenks remained committed to the cause of organic farming, sustainability and environmentalism, and in 1946 he was the co-founder, with Lady Balfour, of the Soil Association. The Transition Towns movement, with its emphasis on local production and localised economies, was anticipated by Jenks in his writings. His last book, *The Stuff Man's Made Of: The Positive Approach to Health through Nutrition*, published in 1959, predated Patrick Holford's *The Optimum Nutrition Bible* by forty years. Jenks died in 1963 of a heart attack, aged 64. Like Budd, it would appear that he may have died overseas, as there is no death certificate recorded for him in this country.[47]

Arnold Leese made an involuntary appearance in Worthing in 1947, along with several other leading members of the Imperial Fascist League, such as Tony Gittens. Seven men in all appeared before local magistrates, charged with harbouring two fugitive Waffen SS soldiers and with supplying them with false passports to enable them to start a new life in Argentina. Initially, the two SS men were sheltered in the New Age premises of Emanuel Alford and his son Leslie in Shoreditch, but following a police raid Leslie helped the two fugitives to clamber over the back wall and escape. They next found refuge at the home of Frederick Edmunds, who lived at 107, Littlehampton Road in Worthing. Edmunds and his wife created a makeshift bedroom for the SS men in their attic, but on December 15th 1946, just days before the pair were due start their journey to Argentina, the police raided the Edmunds' home, and the SS men were captured.[48]

Arnold Leese developed his ant-Semitism while serving with the British Army as a vet in the Middle East during the First World War. He strongly sympathised with the Arab cause and believed that the 'Balfour Declaration' in favour of a Jewish homeland amounted to a betrayal. So extreme were his views that he regarded Mosley as a 'Kosher Fascist'.

At the trial, held at Lewes, Edmunds tried to pretend that the men – who were Dutch nationals – were just friends and that he had no idea they were fugitives or Nazis. Leese, the mastermind of the operation (whose code name was 'the man who likes cats') made no pretence of innocence, demanding to know why he and his co-defendants were on trial while British soldiers were being killed by Jewish fighters in Palestine – the implication of his remarks being that the Jews, not the Nazis, had been Britain's real enemies. He claimed that he had 'hundreds of friends in the East End' who still supported the fascist cause. When asked about his code name, he said that his cat was now a more active fascist than himself and gave the fascist salute before having its dinner. All the defendants were found guilty and sentenced to twelve months' imprisonment – a very modest sentence in the circumstances.[49] Had they committed such acts a few years earlier, during the war, they could have faced the death penalty.

Four years later, Leese published his darkly eccentric biography, *Out of Step: Events in the Two Lives of an Anti-Jewish Camel Doctor.* He died in 1956, aged 78, leaving his substantial London home to Colin Jordan, a young acolyte, who became notorious for his Nazi activities during the 1960s.[50]

Notes and References

1   Wikipedia sites for 'Oswald Mosley' and 'Jorian Jenks'. Also, www.angmeringvillage.co.uk/history/Articles/Jenks.htm

2   Wikipedia sites for 'Arnold Leese', 'Imperial Fascist League', and 'British Fascists'

3   *Worthing Journal*, March 1939, p.7

4   *Worthing Herald*, 30th April, 1932, p.15, *Worthing Herald*, August 13th, 1932, p.11

5   *Worthing Journal*, December 1933, p.16

6   File KV 2/2309, National Archives

7   The author is grateful to Philip Woods for researching the Budd family on Ancestry.com, including the wills. The family appears to have been very wealthy in the early nineteenth century, with Budd's grandfather leaving a substantial sum in his will. This wealth appears to have been greatly reduced by the time that Budd himself inherited. A very impressive monument to the Bentincks, dating from the early nineteenth century, still stands to this day in Brixton.

8   Wikipedia site for 'Jorian Jenks'. Also, www.angemeringvillage.co.uk/history/Articles/Jenks.htm and article by Gordon Blackwell at www.oswaldmosley.com. For more detailed analysis, see: Moore-Colyer, Charles, *Towards 'Mother Earth': Jorian Jenks, the Right and the British Union of Fascists* in *Journal of Contemporary History*, July 2004, Vol. 39, no.3 (University of Aberystwyth 2004).

9   *Worthing Journal*, May 1933, p.6

10   *Worthing Journal*, June 1935, p.1

11   *Worthing Gazette*, 11th October 1933

12   *Worthing Journal*, June 1934, p.14

13   *Worthing Journal*, July 1934, p.4

14   Hare, Chris, *Worthing – Riot and Respectability in a Seaside Town* (Phillimore 2008), p.176

15   *Worthing Journal*, February 1934, p.2

16   Ibid., February 1934, p.11

17 Ibid.

18 *Worthing Herald*, 8th December 1937, Guild Care cuttings file, vol. 1

19 *Worthing Journal*, February 1934, p.3

20 *Worthing Journal*, March 1935

21 *Worthing Journal*, June 1938, p.12

22 *Worthing Journal*, November 1938, p.31

23 Ibid.

24 *Worthing Journal*, March 1940, p.8

25 *Worthing Journal*, May 1937, p.6

26 *Worthing Journal*, December 1938, p.26

27 Author in conversation with Michael Payne, author of *Storm Tide – Worthing: Prelude to War 1933 – 1939* (Verite CM Limited 2008 & 2010)

28 *Worthing Journal*, September 1939, p.8

29 *Worthing Journal*, November 1939, p.3

30 *Worthing Journal*, January 1940, p.6

31 *Worthing Journal*, February 1940, p.5

32 *Worthing Journal*, March 1940, p.5

33 *Worthing Journal*, July 1940, p.1

34 *Worthing Journal*, January 1940, p.19

35 *Worthing Journal*, April 1940, p.13

36 *Worthing Herald*, 27th June, 1941, p.1

37 Winterton, Rt. Hon. Earl, *Orders of the Day* (Cassell and Company 1953), p.15

38 *Worthing Journal*, June 1940, p.3

39 *Worthing Herald*, May 1940

40 See *Worthing Herald* for May 7th, p.2; June 13th, p.12; July 11th, p.1 – all 1941

41 File KV 2/2311, National Archives

42 File KV 2/2313, National Archives

43 File KV 2/2310, National Archives

44 Hansard (House of Lords), Vol. 130, 25th January 1944, pp 487 – 516

45 File KV 2/2312, National Archives

46 Author in conversation with Les Grout, c.1988

47 Research by Phil Wood ibid.

48 'Worthing's Hidden Nazis', article by Chris Hare, *Worthing Review*, 30th November 1990, p.6. *Worthing Gazette*, 14th March, 1947 p.2

49 'Worthing's Hidden Nazis', ibid., *Worthing Gazette*, 4th April 1947, p.9

50 Wikipedia site, 'Arnold Leese'. Colin Jordan formed the National Socialist Movement in 1962, with John Tyndall, who went on to become the leader of the National Front in the 1970s. Nick Griffin, the current leader of the British National Party, was a youth leader in the National Front; so a clear lineage can be established between Arnold Leese and today's 'racial nationalists' in the BNP. However their targets have changed, from Jews in Leese's time, to Blacks in the 1970s, to Muslims today.

6

Getting Ready for War

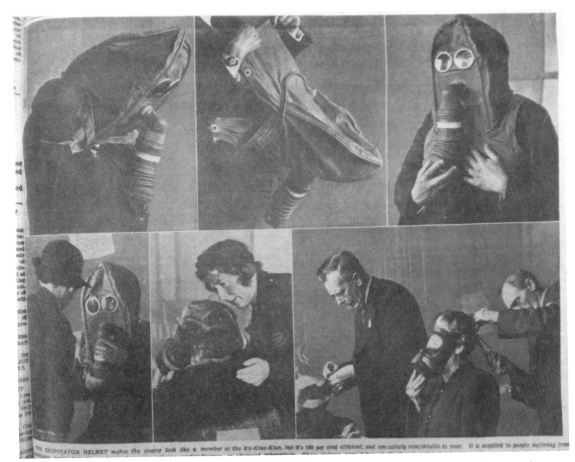

THE RESPIRATOR HELMET makes the wearer look like a member of the Ku-Klux-Klan, but it's 100 per cent efficient, and am azingly comfortable to wear. It is supplied to people suffering from

This rather terrifying set of images appeared in the local Press in 1940 and were designed to reassure the general population as to the utility and effectiveness of gas mask, or 'respirators'. *Reproduced courtesy Johnston Press.*

The preparations for war were not carried out in the last frantic weeks before hostilities broke out in September 1939, but had been underway for several years. As early as May 1935, Worthing Town Council was organising compulsory 'anti-gas training', a necessary response, thought *Autolycus*, 'As the possibility of the reign of King Kong draws steadily nearer.'[1] He followed his pointed reference to Adolf Hitler with the humorous observation that the Council's training sessions on how to deal with a gas attack were been held at the Electricity Showrooms! These public demonstrations were intended to be practical in their application: 'Gas drill is being carried on so realistically', explained *Autolycus*, 'that some volunteers have now an exceedingly good idea of what it feels like to be gassed.'[2] In the event of war, people were instructed to carry their gas mask around with them in a box container, hung by a strap over their shoulder. There were also special masks for small children and babies.

Yet despite this effort to convey the horrors of a gas attack to the wider public, the outbreak of war did not result in mass panic. The greatest annoyance, as far as most people were concerned, was the powers given to the ARP wardens to check that people were in possession of their gas masks, or 'respirators' as they were officially called, and to carry out 'periodical inspections' to ensure that the equipment had not been damaged, lost or misused.[3] Despite the potential threat from the skies and the intrusion of the wardens, a rather lax, even mischievous, attitude began to prevail. In November 1939 *Autolycus* reported to his readers that gas mask cases were becoming very popular for carrying stolen apples[4] – presumably 'scrumped' from orchards by local youths. Jacqueline Simpson [b.1930] remembers that people carried their gas masks around for about six months, 'then they dropped the whole idea.' Dorothy Till [b.1921] recalls carrying food around in her gas mask container, despite the danger of being stopped by a warden –

> *You had to wear them. If you were seen in the street without one, someone would stop you, some warden would stop you. You were supposed to carry it all the time, you see – to the cinema and everything else. I didn't believe in gas masks – I didn't think it could happen. So I used to carry a banana and a bar of chocolate in mine. At the air raid shelter at the back of the Town Hall, I was stuck for five hours [without food] once before the all clear went. I thought, I'm not going to do that again, I'm carrying my food around with me.*

By 1938, the country, including Worthing, was taking the prospect of war so seriously that plans

Dorothy Till has many memories of Worthing in the 1930s and 40s, including her time working with the Land Army during the Second World War. During the 1950s she was a volunteer at Worthing's first Family Planning Clinic, and in the 1960s she was persuaded by Joseph Sayers, Secretary of Worthing and District Council of Social Service, to take the lead role in organising a branch of the Single Woman and her Dependants, an organisation that campaigned for women to receive the same tax breaks as single men did for looking after elderly or disabled relatives. As a married woman, Dorothy may not have seemed to obvious choice for the job, but she had much campaigning experience, and, besides, she was a more suitable choice than the existing secretary – Joseph Sayers! *Reproduced courtesy Malcolm McCluskey, Worthing Herald.*

Jacqueline Simpson's family came to Worthing in the late nineteenth century. Both her grandfather and father were notable figures in the town. Her father was one of the founding members of WCSS in 1933. Jacqueline recalls the life of an upper middle- class family in Worthing before the war, which included servants and strictly observed standards of social etiquette. The war changed this lifestyle dramatically, as she describes both in this book and in *Through the Hard Times and the Good.* Jacqueline is today internationally renowned as an authority on English and Nordic folklore, and is the author of *The Folklore of Sussex*, recently re-published. *Reproduced courtesy of Malcolm McCluskey, Worthing Herald.*

were drawn up for constructing air raid shelters. Despite the seriousness of these precautions, *Autolycus* could not resist applying a dose of black humour to the situation. He was unimpressed by the construction of trenches, designed to hold many hundreds of people, that were dug in early 1939 in the Steyne, Homefield Park, Victoria Park, Manor Sports Ground, Tarring Recreation Ground, Beach House Park, Broadwater Green, and the Cemetery. Surely, he mused, people would prefer to be killed in the comfort of their own homes?[5] In regard to personal air raid shelters, he noted that a survey by the Council had revealed that of 228 basements examined in private houses, only one was found to be suitable for use as an air raid shelter. He wondered if these efforts were not misplaced: 'We used to smile at the idea of Pharaoh spending his life watching the building of his tomb, the Pyramid,' he intoned, 'Now we are advised officially to follow his example and devote ourselves to the building of bomb-proof shelters!'[6]

Autolycus recorded the other preparations for war taking place in the town; among them the big effort to import thousands of sandbags into Worthing. By August 1939, there were 168,000 sandbags stored in the Corporation Depot in High Street (now Markwick's Mews), with 50,000 more on order.[7] Yet here too the *Worthing Journal's* columnist could not resist poking fun at those hoping to make money out of the emergency. He reported that one local firm, hoping to cash in on the crisis, had bought thousands of sandbags, only to discover they were sewn together with ordinary cotton rather than heavy-duty bind, and were, therefore, useless.[8]

Following the declaration of war on 3rd September 1939, the first impact on Worthing was the immediate dispatching of thousands of evacuees to Worthing, mainly from the East End of London. As described in *Through the Hard Times and the Good*, these poor bewildered children received a generally warm welcome, although some of their hosts were shocked by their poverty, lack of manners, and ignorance of hygiene. In the months leading up to war, *Autolycus* raised several doubts about the desirability and effectiveness of the evacuation programme. He demanded to know why middle-class people like himself should be paid 8s 6d (42.5p) for each evacuee child they took into their homes, while an unemployed man would get half that sum to provide for his own children.[9] He also pointed out that Worthing had 1,500 empty properties; why could not these be requisitioned to provide homes for evacuees?[10]

When the evacuees did arrive – over 10,000 during the first weeks of September – there were many in Worthing who were aghast at the condition of the new arrivals. One local councillor described them as 'savages, not as clean as pigs.'[11] *Autolycus* reported, whether satirically or not it is hard to know, that the Evacuation Committee had run out of 'sheep dip', needed to rid the evacuees of fleas.[12] His subsequent comments would certainly not pass the test of modern political correctness, and do appear rather shocking, seventy years on -

> *In mediaeval times, lepers had to carry a bell and cry 'unclean.' For obvious reasons they were not allowed to travel in a bus or train. People up and down the country are talking about the good old days.*[13]

And again –

> *Worthing has long been a place of refuge for outworn doctrines, but the evacuees, with their up-to-date*

ideas from a great city, have proved to the satisfaction of many of us the truth of evolution – that man (and woman) have ascended from the lower animals![14]

No doubt the sheer scale of the influx – the evacuees represented about 15% of the population of the town by the end of September 1939 – in part explains the virulence of these remarks, but they are also a reminder that the fear of outsiders and of things foreign is not confined to the arrival of immigrants from thousands of miles away, but can apply to people who have travelled a distance of no more than seventy miles.

As stated in *Through the Hard Times and the Good*,[15] the middle class saw their living standards fall during the early years of the war, while poorer people benefited from the war economy, which brought full employment and greater state benefits for families and the elderly. Jacqueline Simpson [b.1930], whose father was one of the founding members of Worthing Council of Social Service, remembers how her family had to scale down in 1939, and that, having moved out of 'Heslington', one of the town's most substantial residences, they would never return –

In 1939 my father decided when the war broke out that Heslington House... was much too big to use in wartime, and also we'd been told that we'd have refugees [evacuees] billeted on us from London. So he said that the best thing to do was to move into a smaller house and let Heslington be entirely taken over by refugees. And it was taken over by some nuns and a small school or orphanage or something. That didn't last very long because by 1940 refugees were being taken away from Worthing instead of being sent down here. So it was only for about a year at most that we had these nuns and kids in Heslington. We moved into a house in Christchurch Road where I still live. And originally we rented it thinking we'd go back to Heslington after the war, but we never did go back to Heslington – much too big. My father died. No point – a huge place like that for a family of two.

The threat of invasion, following the Dunkirk debacle of May 1940, made the Sussex coast a very unsafe destination for evacuees, who were subsequently moved to the Midlands and the North of England.

Many of the large houses and villas in Worthing went the same way as Heslington. After the war, many were converted into flats, bedsits, and offices. Still other, more substantial, houses were demolished altogether, such as Offington Hall, The Warren, and Muntham Court. The great house for one family became increasingly anachronistic, in an age where class divisions were breaking down. When, in 1959, Miss Sheila Wrixon-Becher inherited 'Rowdell' at Washington from her late mother, Lady Constance Becher, she decided on the drastic step of demolishing the ancestral home which dated back to medieval times. Her rational was simple: 'It's almost impossible to get domestic help round here,' she complained to a reporter from a local newspaper.[16] Before the war, there were plenty of men and women prepared to 'go into service', but after the war, in an era of full employment, being a servant was not a career option that many would choose. This hiatus of equality did not last of course, and the gap between rich and poor began to widen again from the 1980s onwards. For good or ill, the Second World War proved to be something of a leveller.

One thing that *Autolycus*, writing in the *Journal* during the early months of the war, did approve of was the introduction of petrol rationing, which resulted in 'pedestrians coming into their own

Graham Bishop was, until his retirement in 1989, the town's Borough Engineer. It is thanks to him that the photographs of bomb damage in Worthing that appear in chapter 9 were preserved. Graham found the album while clearing out filing cabinets and cupboards prior to his retirement and realised its historical significance. The album which had been kept by the Council during the war as a record of the impact of enemy action on the town, and he passed it to Worthing Museum for safe keeping. *Reproduced courtesy of Malcolm McCluskey, Worthing Herald*

again.'[17] He remarked on the total tranquillity that now enveloped many rural locations. One correspondent to the *Journal* told how he had made the journey from Guildford to Worthing on Christmas Eve and had not seen another car on the road.[18] This, *Autolycus* thought, must have been a record.

This was the period of the 'Phoney War', but after the fall of France and the Dunkirk evacuation of May 1940, invasion became a real possibility. Graham Bishop [b.1932] clearly remembers life in his Goring home that summer and that visions of German invaders storming up the beaches had an unsettling effect on people, living in what had become by that time an affluent suburb of Worthing –

My father had to stay [because of his job] and it was really quite, quite terrifying at times really, because we knew any moment we could be invaded, and back in August 1940 I well remember a... major came round, an army major, and said that invasion was imminent and people were advised to leave. And that weekend practically everybody left Goring Hall estate; people had their cats and dogs put to sleep and they just went off to stay with friends or made other arrangements and the place was absolutely empty. We had to stay because my father had to stay, but it was eerie. We walked around the estate, there were no lights on, everybody had gone and we kept a full tank of petrol in the car... you expected invasion any day.

Notes and References

1   *Worthing Journal*, June 1935, p.5

2   *Worthing Journal*, October 1937, p.15

3   The local Press carried many news stories and adverts alerting the population to the new regulations. An advert in the *Worthing Journal*, December 1938, p.25, stated that all ARP Wardens and Officials who wore 'spectacles' must get a prescription for a pair of 'official Mark IV gas mask spectacles' and that only these could be with 'Civilian Duty and Service Respirators'. An article in the *Worthing Herald*, 27th March 1940, warned of the penalties for infringing the regulations regarding respirators, and that residents would no longer be able to have their gas masks repaired free of charge, presumably due to a high incidence of damage up until that time.

4   *Worthing Journal*, November 1939, p.3

5   *Worthing Journal*, March 1939, p.10

6   *Worthing Journal*, June 1938, p.12

7   *Worthing Journal*, September 1939, p.18

8   *Worthing Journal*, April 1939, p.11

9   *Worthing Journal*, March 1939, pp 9-10

10   Ibid., p.9

11   *Worthing Journal*, November 1939, p.5

12   Ibid. p.8

13   Ibid., p..7

14   Ibid.,pp 7-8

15   Hare, Chris, *Through the Hard Times and the Good – an oral and social history of Worthing* (Guild Care 2009), pp 47 -49

16   Hare, Chris, *The Washington Story – the forgotten history of a downland village* (Washington Parish Council 2000), p.11. Miss Wrixon-Becher had the Rowdell stable block converted into her new home, and this was all that survived of a country house that dated back to at least 1312, when it was first mentioned in an extant document.

17   *Worthing Journal*, November 1939, p.5

18   *Worthing Journal*, February 1940, p.6

Opposite: Members of Worthing Home Guard gather on Broadwater Green during the war. Broadwater Green was a regular meeting place for the various Worthing Home Guard platoons, being a larger enough area for training and parades. The Home Guard, or Local Defence Volunteers, as they were originally known, was 'stood down' in 1944, before the end of the war, once the threat of invasion had abated. *Reproduced courtesy Worthing Museum.*

7

Home Guard and Land Army

The Home Guard march down South Street on manoeuvres during the early years of the war. The image of discipline and organisation conveyed by pictures such as these belied the stark reality: had the Germans invaded, the Home Guard would have been overwhelmed and probably massacred by the superior firepower of the invaders. *Reproduced courtesy of Johnston Press.*

With Britain facing a real danger of imminent invasion in 1940, every adult in the country was expected to make their contribution to the war effort. For many younger people, this meant joining the Armed Forces. For others, who were older (or were in what were known as 'Reserved Occupations') there were other options, including the Local Defence Volunteers (LDV), or for women, the Land Army. Men aged between 17 and 20 were also eligible for the LDV, although later in the war even these younger men were sent to fight overseas.

The LDV soon become known as the Home Guard, but for many people who grew up with the popular 1960s and 70s TV comedy series it will forever be remembered as *Dad's Army*. Despite the enduring image of the elderly and frequently bumbling characters from the TV series, most Home Guard volunteers were in their 30s rather than their 70s. No men aged over 41 were conscripted for active service overseas and no men of any age in a reserved occupation were called up. These occupations included mining, engineering, but also certain retail trades as well. Women between the ages of 21 and 30 were eligible to serve in the Land Army, taking over the duties of men who had been called up. In 1942 men up to the age of 51 became eligible for war work. In Worthing in 1941 the oldest recruit was reported to be 77-year-old Arthur Lowe of 37 Gordon Road (yes, he really did have the same name as the actor who later went on to play Captain Mainwaring in *Dad's Army*).[1]

The Home Guard was supposed to be the first line of defence in the event of a German invasion. Had the invasion taken place, confidential papers released after the war suggest that the poorly equipped and trained part-time soldiers would have been overwhelmed, suffering massive casualties. Regular forces were supposed to hold the line north of the Downs, while special forces would operate from underground bunkers, launching sabotage raids and guerrilla warfare. How this would have worked out in practice we cannot know, but we can probably assume that every south coast town today would have a memorial to the Home Guard men killed resisting the invasion, and that each memorial would have been inscribed with hundreds of names. The fact that this catastrophe did not occur allows us to look back on the Home Guard with humour and affection, rather than sorrow and regret.[2]

Syd Ede [b.1914] worked at the market gardens at Thakeham during the war, and used to make the journey every day from his Worthing home by bicycle. It was hard work and the journey was a round trip of nearly 20 miles, but there was no peaceful night's sleep for Syd, who had to go on sentry duty with the Home Guard at night. Although he was supposed to sleep between the two-hour sentry shifts, he never could, but stayed up talking with the men on the next shift. They had very little ammunition, which each shift had to unload from their old Lee Enfield rifles and pass on to the next group of men. Having emptied his magazine, each man was then supposed to pull the trigger on his rifle, in upwards position, to make sure there was no bullet left in the chamber. They were stationed close to Splash Point and had a small guard room. The upper floor was used by the commanding officer, a retired Naval Captain, who, following one unfortunate incident, was lucky to escape with his life, as Syd recalls –

We had five rounds of ammo. We had rifles, so we was well armed – Lee Enfield – and when you were on duty you had the five rounds – you put them in – then a chap came off duty, he unloaded them and then you put them in your gun. Well, we had one chap there, Ken Bruce – Ken, young Ken, he was only a youngster, and he came off duty one night and he [was] supposed to unload see, and then you fire the gun so it was clean. Well Ken couldn't have, he left one [cartridge] in, and he – I'll never forget – he fired this rifle, mind you, it was in the house, and we had an old, God knows what he was going there, an old army Captain; well he was old but he had a young nurse – used to sleep with her upstairs, and when Ken pulled the [trigger], the shot went up through the ceiling and there was a hell of a noise upstairs and the language was terrible! But I never forget this

Syd Ede, who served in the Home Guard, has some entertaining memories of his experiences on sentry duty in 1940. *Reproduced courtesy Malcolm McCluskey, Worthing Herald.*

captain – Captain Biggins, that's right,
Captain Biggins – retired naval chap – he came
storming downstairs, and apparently he was
asleep – well on the bed – and this bullet went
up the skirting – the wall, and up through the
ceiling and his bed.

Some were not so lucky. Ron Pierce [b.1922] was training with the Findon Home Guard on Nepcote Green, where they were being instructed in how to use a Bren gun. The army instructor was showing the men how to make the gun safe, but in taking off the magazine, he pulled the trigger, firing the bullet that was still in the breach into Ron's knee. This type of accident was not uncommon: a year later a Home Guard instructor was shot dead in similar circumstances.[3]

In echoes of *Dad's Army*, Marjorie Pressley [b.1916] remembers that her older brother, Arthur, was promoted to the rank of Sergeant because he was a butcher, and could supply the men with fresh meat. This unorthodox method of selection caused some consternation when the Home Guard trained with regular soldiers –

....well they used to do their training on
Sundays when the shops were closed and the
men were free, and he went up on the hills for
grenade practice, and under a regular soldier, a
regular sergeant. And this regular sergeant
said to Arthur, you know, could he take some of
these chaps to teach them and Arthur said no,
he'd never used the grenade... so he [the regular
sergeant] said, 'Well, how did you get your
stripes?' He said, 'I'm the battalion butcher!

Alan Townsend [b.1925] served in the Home Guard before joining the regular army. He remembers the Home Guard HQ at Muir House – now demolished – which used to stand in Broadwater Road, opposite St Mary's church.

A Home Guard Battalion marches over the old Broadwater Road bridge across the railway. Alan Townsend remembers that his battalion was responsible for the destruction of several lampposts in Broadwater Road in 1940, due to their unorthodox approach to establishing communication links with their HQ at Muir House. *Reproduced courtesy of West Sussex County Library Service* – www.westsussexpicturespast.org.uk

GHOST HAUNTS HOME GUARD HEADQUARTERS

NEARLY every night for the last week or so the clump-clump of heavy boots has re-echoed up the uncarpeted s t a i r s and through the empty corridors of a certain ancient Worthing house, which

Innocent Home Guard men have been called over the coals for disturbing the midnight rest of senior officers—and have been able to prove that they've never moved.

The mysterious visitor has been heard by most of the headquarters staff at one time or another—from senior administra-

a friendly interest in their very own ghost, and if only he can be persuaded to materialise they're going to put him on the strength, provided he is of English parentage!

A "Herald" reporter, who se out to discover whether the house in question had ever before housed a ghost, sought the aid of Miss Ethel Gerard, Worthing's

Tug Wilson remembers the ghost that supposedly haunted the main Home Guard HQ at Candia in Lyndhurst Road. It is not known it the ghost still inhabits the building today, now used as the headquarters for the St. John's Ambulance. *Reproduced courtesy of Johnston Press.*

One of their responsibilities was to set up communications between the various Home Guard look-out and sentry posts dotted around the town. Alan remembers that they were not very competent in this task, and even 'borrowed' wire from the Canadian soldiers in the town when they ran out of their own supply –

And we had a telephone exchange there [at Muir House], and we could connect the look-outs and the gun-points – connect them all together with this. And I remember one day we were up on Lloyds Bank there on South Street, and one of our chaps slipped and fell through the two floors of the bank. And we all got arrested. 'Home Guard Yobbos' I think it said in the 'paper.... And we were stringing up along Broadwater [Road] – before the road was widened – and there were these old metal lampposts – the iron ones – and a 'bus came along, caught one of the wires and pulled about six lamp posts with it. And we got into trouble over that. We were looked upon with a bit of a frown I think. We used to wait for the Canadians to lay their cable down and then we'd go and reel it up because we couldn't get any of our own, you see. We used to wait for them to reel this out and we'd go and pick it up.

The local population may not have felt entirely confident in the capabilities of the Home Guard. *Autolycus* warned his readers in July 1940 to be careful when approaching one of their sentry points: 'On the whole it is safer to stand still and shout 'Friend', and not to hesitate when told to advance for recognition. If even partly deaf don't go near guarded places alone.'[4]

Tug Wilson [b 1927] was based at the town's other main Home Guard HQ, Candia, in Lyndhurst Road. This is where the Home Guard armoury was kept, including mines. Many of the men stationed there at night were convinced that the house was haunted. Despite reassurances from Ethel Gerard, the Curator of Worthing Museum, that there was no history of ghostly activity at Candia and that 'without exception' all the previous occupants had been 'most respectable people'[5] (implying only the disreputable lingered on as ghosts), Home Guard sentries heard strange sounds during the night that they could not explain. An artist, who had lived in the house some years earlier, wrote to the local Press, saying that he too had experienced strange sensations in the house.[6] Tug Wilson remembers going to investigate one winter's night –

> *I heard noises in the night, so, er, I went down with fixed bayonet. I don't know what that would have done, I'm sure but.... [I] opened the door downstairs with the bayonet and, erm, the noises stopped, and I, erm, to get there I had stepped over about eight people sleeping on the floor, but seeing as I was the only one awake, I'd go down and investigate. And when I came back they all said, 'What was that down there?' .... It was just noises, like a child crying... [later on] I used to think it was probably an owl or something, I don't know....*

Young unmarried women could join the female sections of the Armed Forces, such as the WRENS, or they could take up other forms of war work, such as working in munitions factories or the Land Army. Dorothy Till [b.1921] swapped her suburban life for one in the country at Tote Hill Farm north of Pulborough, and it proved to be something of a culture shock –

Three 'land girls' arrive at Worthing Station to take up their roles in the Land Army. One of our interviewees, Mary Martin, recognised Iris Parvin, on the left, as her cousin from Brighton, Iris Parvin. The two other women shown are Betty Daniels and Barbara Paine. *Reproduced courtesy of Johnston Press.*

These women appear to be enjoying themselves feeding this huge pig, but not all those who served in the Land Army enjoyed the experience, including Gladys Ede, who was assaulted and suffered a serious injury. *Reproduced courtesy Johnston Press.*

I lived in Browning Road, where we have always had hot water, we had central heating, we had electricity – and I'm shoved in a farm which had no electricity, no gas – had to go to bed with a candle, to cook with a Primus Stove, with methylated spirit in it; had to go out in the yard and pump water up with a pump, and take your chamber pot in the morning and tip it in the Arun. Imagine!

Gladys Ede [b.1921] worked at a farm near Slindon with other Lands Girls, where she fed horses, calves, chickens, and the farm dogs. All went well until she was told to take on milking duties from the cowgirl who was away on a short holiday –

I lived in the farmhouse with the farmer and his wife – they were a young couple and we lived very well actually. We had a very nice room – bedrooms and a bathroom to ourselves and we had lovely food and lots of cream. We were lucky.... I was only there four months actually, 'cause one morning the cowgirl was off for the weekend and they asked me to help very early in the morning and I had never done it before. They had a moveable milking shed in the field and each day it would be moved to a fresh plot and it was all done by electric milking machines and she told me to put the cups on the cow and I did it the wrong way round and she kicked me, she kicked me up the bottom and I am afraid she injured me and that was the end of my thing.

After this violent conclusion to her career in farming, Gladys went to work on the market gardens in East Worthing, where she met Dorothy Till, who was also working there by that time. As detailed in a later chapter of this book, both women were very lucky to escape with their lives when the nurseries were attacked by a 'tip 'n' run' raider.

Notes and References

1   *Worthing Herald*, 15th August 1941, p.15

2   Please see 'further reading' for books dealing with this subject. The true consequences of a German invasion were first revealed locally in the *Worthing Herald*, 26th November 1946, p.1, when in a response to a written parliamentary question, the Prime Minister, Clement Atlee, revealed that an invasion had been expected at 8pm on September 7th, 1940. The local population would have been evacuated to woods to the north of the town. The Coldstream Guards would have retreated to the second line of defence, leaving the Home Guard to 'fight to the death.'

3   *Worthing Herald*, 21st August 1941 , p.8

4   *Worthing Journal*, July 1940, p.4

5   *Worthing Herald*, 24th January 1941, p.1

6   *Worthing Herald*, 31st January 1941, p.1

8

The Canadians in Worthing

Fraternisation between local women and soldiers always caused a certain amount of tension in the town, but this anxiety appears to have increased when the soldiers in question were Canadian and especially when they were French Canadians. These tensions not infrequently manifested themselves in violent incidents in the town. *Reproduced courtesy Johnston Press.*

For much of the Second World War troops were stationed in Worthing, with numbers rising prior to the Dieppe Raid in August 1942 and D-Day in June 1944. Many of these soldiers were Canadians, and their presence in the town is still a source of some controversy. While some people remember them with affection, others have recollections of drunkenness, fighting and even sexual assault. The Press during the war, although censored, gave a clear indication that the relationship between the Canadian soldiers and the locals was, at best, an uneasy one. Was this another example – as with the evacuees – of a reaction to a large influx of outsiders? Were the Canadians really any more badly behaved than British troops stationed in the town? It is noticeable that many of those interviewed for this project drew a distinction between the 'English' Canadians and the French Canadians, as seen in these comments by Teri Noice [b.1920] –

> .... A lot of people run down the Canadians. And the Three River Boys at Maple Leaf weren't anything to do with the French Canadians. And it was the French Canadians that caused all the trouble in Worthing, but, they – people just say Canadians. So they also got the bad, bad name. But they weren't anything, they didn't do anything like that. It was only the French Canadians that did all the trouble.

Over the years a degree of legend or mythology has grown up around the activities of Canadian and particularly French Canadian troops in Worthing. It has been claimed that 'They would tie local girls to lamp posts and rape them,'[1] and that fights in local pubs between Canadians and British soldiers were so violent that there were fatalities on both sides, with both guns and knives being used as weapons.

The Press reports for the wartime years in Worthing certainly do indicate that there were violent clashes in the town, although not on the scale recalled by some people, where the passing of decades may have allowed imagination to mingle with fact. Where Canadians were involved in trouble, the surnames of those accused were as likely to be typically English or Irish as French. A fight on Worthing seafront on Christmas Eve 1941 led to the arrest of Private Russell McBurney, who was given three months' hard labour for assaulting Police Constable House in the execution of his duty. Later that same evening, Private James Dennis Chamberlin was shot dead by a sentry and another Canadian was wounded, when they returned from a drunken spree. The sentry claimed to have fired by mistake while he was lowering his rifle to put the safety catch on.[2] Over time, perhaps these two

ASSAULT ON SIX POLICE OFFICERS

Soldiers Had To Be Put In Leg Irons

AFTER three Canadian soldiers had fought with six Worthing police-constables at the George Hotel car park Superintendent Lewis pleaded with the magistrates at Worthing Police Court on Tuesday: "They are very sorry indeed. I am convinced their action was due to drink."

The local police were sometimes stretched in trying to deal with the presence of large numbers of soldiers in the town and were often called upon to deal with pub brawls that had spilled out onto the streets. Not surprisingly soldiers were most tense when waiting to go on active service, such as the Dieppe Raid in 1942 or D-Day in 1944. *Reproduced courtesy Johnston Press.*

incidents, separate but occuring on the same night, may have been conflated into one event, with soldiers being shot dead at the seafront brawl?

A fight outside the George Hotel earlier the same year, between Canadian soldiers and the police, also attracted considerable coverage in the Worthing newspapers. Three Canadians were arrested as a result of the brawl. There surnames were, Keeley, Kesler, and Ferguson, none of which sound very French – Kesler sounds as if it could be German or Nordic in origin. Following this incident, six Canadians were put in leg-irons to restrain them. It is also interesting that Superintendent Lewis pleaded with the magistrates to be lenient with the men, explaining: 'They are very sorry indeed. I am convinced their action was due to drink.' On this occasion the three defendants were fined rather than imprisoned.[3]

A more serious incident occurred at the Mulberry Hotel in January 1942. Canadian soldier George Bertrand fired into the bar, wounding one of the customers, William Wood. He then pointed his gun at a girl standing in the car park, until he was overpowered by Company Sergeant Major Murdoch. Bertrand, who probably was of French descent, was sentenced to three months' hard labour. The magistrate, Mr W. Healey, commented that too many Canadian soldiers were getting out of hand and this sort of thing must be stopped.[4]

One former mayor felt that too much emphasis was being placed on the ethnic origin of soldiers being arrested and that unsolved crimes were blamed on Canadians without evidence: 'I know the Canadians haven't a good name,' he pleaded, 'but give them a chance.' Unfortunately, in March 1942, this same man, who asked the Press not to print his name – for he feared reprisals – was waylaid one night by two Canadian soldiers, who blocked his path as he walked along the blacked-out streets, as he later recounted to a reporter –

.... One of them stepped right in front of me and the other closed in on me. I asked them what they wanted. They only muttered a reply and one of them grabbed at my case. I snatched it away and pushed it in front of me and dived forward. As I did so I was struck a violent blow behind the ear which knocked me to the ground. I felt I was going to lose consciousness. Simultaneously with the blow on the head I was struck on the arm. I got up not knowing whether I was going to be hit again. The two men had gone. I picked up my hat but I could not find my glasses and I can scarcely see without them. I telephoned the Police and one of them used his torch to search for my glasses, which he found after twenty minutes.[5]

When the shaken man arrived home, his daughter reported to him that she had been followed home and 'pestered' by a Canadian soldier. Bob Copper [b.1915] was a policeman in Worthing during the war, and recalled the incidents in the town involving the Canadian troops. He explained that many soldiers had been released from prison sentences on the understanding that they would enlist, and that some of those who got into conflict with the police and the general population in Worthing were of this type. He also fondly recalled the men of the Royal Canadian Mounted Police ('Mounties'), whose job it was to keep order in the ranks – 'They were a wonderful bunch of blokes, they really were. Great men, great men.'

The Mounties were all made honorary members of the Worthing Police Social Club, and Bob became firm friends with one of them, a man by the names of Hawkes, with whom he used regularly to play snooker. When, later in the war, Bob was called to a gas leak in a bungalow in Poulter's Lane, which had been requestioned by the Mounties, he found that a man had collapsed on the inside of the door, and he had to force his way in, pushing the man aside as he entered the property. To his horror, not only was the man dead, but he proved to be his friend Hawkes. Bob saw worse sights than this during the war, but as he said, 'that's the sort of thing you had to put up with.' These were not ordinary times.

Worthing policeman Bob Copper had many fond memories of the Canadians, particularly the 'Mounties'. Bob later became well-known as a folk singer and folk song collector and the author of several books on country life.
Reproduced courtesy Worthing Museum.

Trouble in Worthing pubs did not arrive with the Canadians, Bob remembered, and had been prevalent before the war, when much of the blame was placed on the Welsh and Irish, who had come to Worthing during the Great Depression looking for work. But the presence of soldiers in large numbers added another dimension. As Ernie Blackman [b.1929] recalls, many of the soldiers in Worthing during the 1940s were 'keyed up', knowing that any moment they could be sent on a raid or even the invasion of occupied France. When drink was added to the tension experienced by all fighting men, it is not surprising that there could be fights in the town's pubs. The police in Worthing had to deal with these situations as they arose, although one pub famous for its fights – The Fountain in Chapel Road – became a lot calmer during the war years than it had been in the 30s. Here Bob Copper describes policing the Worthing pubs and their unruly customers in khaki –

> ... you knew the trouble spots where they used to go, it was only too much drink, they were quite decent blokes, I'm sure, when they were sober. But of course they wanted a fight. So we used to bring in the men from the quieter beats and from 9 o'clock you'd go in and pair up with a bloke....[and go to] the troubled pubs.... And of course when they came out [drunk] you'd pick them up – you tried to keep it quiet, but a lot of them were out for trouble, that was their fun, you know. I always remember, it's funny, when people say 'police brutality' – there's nobody less pugilistic than me, and I always used to say, 'Now look here, old son, don't mess about, be a good lad, do us both a good turn, go home quietly', and then you'd get, 'Now look, calm down, push off, be quiet and get out of my sight', and then bump, they'd hurt you, and you think, 'Right!' – and they'd be all, 'oh, you've drawn blood!' It's alright being calm until you get hurt! That's not in the rules. Police brutality is usually in return for brutality anyway. So we did have trouble.

> I mention The Fountain, and that was the busiest pub, there was the least trouble there than any in Worthing and the reason for that was that old Len Neigh had been called up – the landlord – and the licence had reverted to his mother who had had it for years before – and she was a lovely...., very gentle, very smart, used to sit in the corner on the customers' side in the saloon bar, sit with a glass of something, and they'd come in, all the trouble-makers we knew, and they'd be as quiet as mice. If they raised their voices, she'd say, 'Boys, boys' – 'Alright, Mother' they'd say, and there was less trouble there than there was anywhere else. That feminine touch and that dignified, like a duchess – and the Canadian, real rough, backwoods Canadians – a tough lot, and they'd say, 'Sorry Ma'am.

Jacqueline Simpson [b.1930] remembered that on one occasion the family found a Canadian soldier lying fast asleep in the spare bedroom, having entered the house in the middle of the night and now sleeping off his hangover. The door to the house had not been locked and he had let himself in and simply gone to sleep. She also recalls how Canadian soldiers, billeted in a house opposite the Sion Convent (where Jacqueline went to school), used to amuse themselves by shining mirrors across the road and onto the ceiling of the classroom opposite, much to the delight of the children. The nuns in charge of the school complained to the soldiers' commanding officers and the fun was soon stopped.

The attack on the former Worthing mayor, already referred to, certainly increased the mood of hostility and anxiety in the town towards the Canadian troops. There was much correspondence in the Press, particularly concerning the alleged intimidation suffered by the town's women. These comments were made by men, whose anxiety concerning the presence of so many soldiers in the town may have heightened their sense of the threat posed to their wives and girlfriends. One businessman complained: 'It is not only that women are accosted after the black out. I have seen them accosted during the day when out shopping.' However, another man believed that some of the young women were equally to blame for this apparent moral decline: 'It is true that women in the town are frequently pestered by soldiers. At the same time I have been appalled at the sight of some girls – some of them only in their early teens – hanging around billets and public houses. These girls help to encourage the soldiers and make the town unsafe for decent women.'[6] Lady Winterton, wife of the town's MP, took up this issue, although adopting a less condemnatory tone. She felt that it was up to the town's youth organisations to safeguard the vulnerable: 'Young girls of thirteen and fourteen must be protected,' she avowed, 'from soldiers whose wives may be some 3,000 miles away.'[7]

Mrs Ida Wardle and her daughter pose outside their home, 22 St. Wilfred's Road, with three soldiers – one Canadian and two English. The Canadian, 'Jimmy', is in the centre of the photograph. It was this type of friendly concern for soldiers in the town that led to unpleasant rumours and Sergeant Campbell's indignant letter, published in the *Worthing Gazette* in 1942, in which he condemned "wicked contemptible gossip".

Reproduced courtesy West Sussex County Library Service
– www.westsussexpicturespast.org.uk

Rumours were rife in the town concerning women that 'went with soldiers' and these rumours grew more virulent when the soldiers in question happened to be Canadians. It would seem that some of the women who worked at Worthing Hospital were on friendly terms with the Canadian soldiers, and just how 'friendly' they were was the subject of much scandalised gossip. Sergeant Campbell, one of the Canadian soldiers, was so angry about these rumours and the generally hostile attitude of Worthing people towards his countrymen that he wrote a letter of complaint to the *Worthing Gazette* –

Some time ago a local lady and her daughter were kind enough to invite myself and several of my friends to visit their home any time we wished for a cup of tea and a chat. My friends and I availed ourselves of this opportunity, and have visited these two ladies once or twice a week since then. The result of the hospitality offered to us has been wicked contemptible gossip by some of the natives of these parts concerning the visits of Canadian soldiers to these two people. In consequence, our hostesses have been greatly embarrassed. Personally, I consider it a pretty rotten thing for the local inhabitants to have nothing better to do with their time, and no better way of fighting the war, than to spread malicious slander about two women who have shown a little kindness to men who have voluntarily given up everything they had in the world to come and fight for England – and, incidentally, Worthing. The hospitality we have encountered in Worthing has been, to put it mildly, meagre. And now we find that when we are invited into people's homes, it causes a lot of talk. Some town![8]

Sergeant Campbell's letter was countered by the Rev. Barnard Spaull, the Congregational minister at the Shelley Road church and a senior figure in the Worthing Council of Social Service (and, after the War, its chairman). Spaull complained that his congregation had tried everything they could to make the Canadians feel at home, inviting them to folk dancing sessions, snooker matches, and meals, but received a very poor response. Spaull felt it was now up to the Canadians to show a positive spirit and accept the hand of friendship that had been offered to them.[9] Whatever Spaull's concerns, many of those interviewed for this book do remember the Canadians being involved in entertainments in the town, putting on shows at the Pier Pavilion. Eileen Wright [b.1931] remembers the French Canadians

Canadian soldiers, wearing protective jackets, place barbed wire along Marine Parade in 1940 as part of the town's defences against invasion. *Reproduced courtesy West Sussex County Library Service –* www.westsussexpicturespast.org.uk

with fondness: 'There used to be lots of French Canadians on the seafront, near the hotels, and as a child I used to play with them down there, and my sister. And they were as good as gold. It was a really good time.'

Early Winterton, the town's MP, who never did anything by halves, but on occasion spoke with a bluntness that many found rude or offensive, was no less forceful over the matter of the Canadians. His public statement that anyone who attacked Canadians or Canada would be his undying enemy put the lid on the bubbling indignation that had been brewing in the town.[10] Shortly afterwards, over two thousand Canadians were killed in the ill-conceived Dieppe Raid. Many of the Canadians billeted in Worthing never returned. Mary Martin [b.1934], whose mother had befriended a young Canadian soldier, terrified of going to war, remembered that many of the soldiers gave her mother their personal possessions, such as watches, before they went on the Raid, hoping to collect them on their return. But none of them returned and Mary's mother took the poignant items to the Town Hall, not wishing to keep them. 'They were', Mary remembers, 'all very young.'

Difficulties and discipline problems with soldiers, including Canadians, continued throughout the war years. Ron Pierce [b.1922] remembered that his father worked at the gardens at Highden (now

Two Canadian soldiers teach a civilian to roller-skate at Hewitt's Fair, which was situated where the Grafton car park and bowling alley now stands on Marine Parade. The fair, which opened in 1934, remained open through out the war years and closed in 1951. *Reproduced courtesy West Sussex County Library Service – www.westsussexpicturespast.org.uk*

Windlesham House School) at Washington, and one day a Canadian soldier lobbed a grenade over the wall of the garden in which Ron's father was working – he only narrowly escaped being killed. Despite this incident, Ron's father remained on friendly terms with the Canadian soldiers camped on the Downs close by and even sold them produce from the Highden gardens.

In the run-up to D-Day, in June 1944, there was a determined effort to impose the maximum discipline on troops as it was vital that the invasion plans should be kept secret and that the troops should be focused on the great struggle that lay ahead. Those soldiers arrested for criminal activities at this time could expect to face the harshest punishments. Two Canadian soldiers, Andrian Langlais and Raphael Ruschianski, who were convicted of violent robbery, were, in addition to imprisonment, sentenced to be birched.[11]

In 1968, when Dr Gusterson, along with Worthing and District Council of Social Service, was raising funds to build a Hospice in Worthing, he appealed directly to former Canadian soldiers who had been stationed in Worthing. Pete Lock [b.1924] recalls that the Hospice was to be built on land where the Canadians had been based, so Dr Gusterson got in touch with members of the Nova Scotia regiment that had been stationed there, 'and told them what we were doing there, and that Canadians must have received lots of comfort from the Worthing ladies and would they like to contribute to the Hospice?' Pete remembers that there was a very generous response, and that when the Hospice was opened, a plaque was unveiled recording all those Canadians who had donated to the project. As well as the St Barnabas Hospice – recently relocated to Titnore Lane – all the 'Canadian' road names in West Durrington are a permanent reminder of the presence of the servicemen who travelled thousands of miles to fight for Britain and the Empire over seventy years ago.

Notes and References

1 *Worthing Review*, 6th October 1989, p.6, article by Chris Hare, 'More Wartime Memories'
2 *Worthing Gazette*, 31st December 1941, p.5
3 *Worthing Herald*, 4th July 1941
4 *Worthing Gazette*, 7th January 1942, p.5
5 *Worthing Gazette*, 18th March, 1942
6 Ibid.
7 Ibid., p.5
8 *Worthing Gazette*, 1st April 1942, p.7
9 *Worthing Gazette*, 8th April 1942, p.5
10 *Worthing Gazette*, 25th March 1942, p.5
11 *Worthing Gazette*, 15th March 1944

Opposite: Earl Winterton in later years, after he had stepped down as MP for Worthing. His plain speaking and honest assessment about the brutality of war did not always endear him to people wishing to hear good news. His warning, in 1942, that the war was unlikely to end quickly, but would probably continue until 1945, although entirely accurate, did not go down well with a local audience desperate to see loved ones in the Armed Forces return home safely and as soon as possible.

9

Under Attack!

Worthing's plain-speaking patrician MP, Earl Winterton, never left the people of the town in any doubt as to the true meaning of war. As mentioned in a previous chapter, he had exalted the young to 'kill all the Germans you can', and when his uncompromising approach was questioned by some of the town's clergy, he defended himself in a forthright manner. Winterton had served in the trenches during the First World War and knew that war was a bloody and terrible business, and he was determined that the people of Worthing should not be shielded from its reality –

The object of a national war must be to kill as many as possible of the enemy's forces, and to smash the means of existence and subsistence of the general population. That is why war is so brutal and terrible a thing, and is only justifiable (as in the case of the present conflict) because of the awful alternative of the complete enslavement of all of us if Hitler should win.[1]

Winterton's rigorous honesty also extended to refusing to pretend the war might be over quickly. When a number of prominent citizens in the town, including the mayor, expressed the view in early 1942 that the war might end that year, or in 1943 at the latest, Winterton rebuked them as 'foolish people'. While paying tribute to the town's high morale, he nonetheless warned his audience at a public meeting that in his opinion the war would last until 1945 and that future casualties were bound to be 'very large indeed'.[2] This assessment unsettled many in the town, including local JP and youth worker, Sidney Walter, who joined the mounting chorus of disapproval against Winterton's remarks. 'I don't believe,' declared Walter, '[that] the end is so far away as some people think.'[3] Winterton, of course, was spot-on on in his predictions, however unwelcome they may have been at the time.

Unlike modern politicians, Winterton thought nothing of lambasting his electorate, as well as the town's worthies. Having been asked to attend a fund-raising event for National Airborne Week, he found himself unimpressed by the public response, describing the participants as a 'small and apathetic crowd', which looked 'as if it was attending a funeral.'[4] No doubt, there were some in Worthing who breathed a sigh of relief, when, following the division of the Worthing and Horsham constituency in 1945, Winterton decided to seek re-election for Horsham, rather than for Worthing. He continued as an MP until 1955, notching up 51 years in the House of Commons, making him the longest serving MP at the time and 'Father of the House'.

The belief in 'total war' gripped the general population, few of whom questioned the need to see the struggle through to the bitter end. Even Stalin's Soviet Union, guilty of at least as many atrocities as Nazi Germany, was to be embraced: 'Our hearts go out to our brave Russian allies,'[5] intoned Winterton. Much of the hatred of war was directed against Hitler himself, as evidenced in the 'rat' advert run in Worthing's local newspapers. This hatred and desire for vengeance filtered down to the younger generation, as shown by the following extract from a schoolboy's essay, in which he imagines the gruesome punishments that could be inflicted on the Nazi leader after his capture –

> If Hitler was captured the best death for him would be dreadful torture. The best way to make him die would be to put him in plaster of Paris and make him suffer such agony that he would be glad to be out of it. His hair would be set alight and it would be all burned off. His moustache would be singed off his face...every day a bit would be taken off him. Of what remains then when he is half dying would be torn out with pincers and executed.[6]

The experience of being bombed and seeing loved ones killed obviously united people in both grief and in a determination to continue fighting the war until victory was secured. Between 1940 and 1944, casualties in Worthing included 44 killed and 216 injured and wounded. To this number can be added airmen, both German and British, who were killed in Worthing, their planes having been shot down or crashed due to technical faults. There does not appear to be an official figure for these fatalities, but they totalled no fewer than 18. Press censorship during the war often excluded such information, especially if the deaths occurred on the Allied side. As well as the deaths, 650 properties were damaged, either by bombing or from enemy machine-gun and cannon fire. All these incidents were the result of enemy bombing or 'tip 'n' run' raids. Other south coast towns fared worse than Worthing – 198 people were killed in Brighton, while the naval port of Portsmouth suffered far greater losses, at it was targeted by the Luftwaffe.[7]

Although the town had many public air raid shelters, these tended to be used in the event of an air raid warning during the day, when people were in the streets, shopping, or at work. When raids came at night or when people were at home during the day they had to rely on either an Anderson Shelter or a Morrison Shelter to keep them safe. The former was an outdoor, garden shelter, named after the Secretary of State for War, and the latter, an indoors shelter, named after the Home Secretary. Many of the people interviewed for this book tended to have small yards rather than gardens, so the Morrison

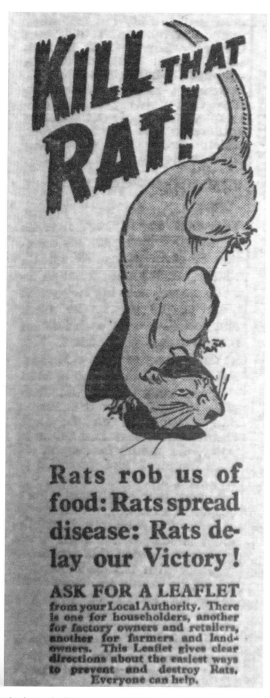

KILL THAT RAT!

Rats rob us of food: Rats spread disease: Rats delay our Victory!

ASK FOR A LEAFLET

from your Local Authority. There is one for householders, another for factory owners and retailers, another for farmers and land-owners. This Leaflet gives clear directions about the easiest ways to prevent and destroy Rats. Everyone can help.

The hatred of Germany, which became almost universal once the bombs started to drop in civilian areas was focused on the personality of the German leader. This local advert, encouraging people to kill rats, gives the rodent a distinctly Hitler-like appearance. *Reproduced courtesy Johnston Press.*

Shelter was the only option for them. These shelters were like very large metal tables, surrounded with wire netting, under which the household would seek refuge. During the London Blitz, when bombers were passing over on a nightly basis, many families slept in their shelters every night.

Graham Bishop's [b. 1932] family lived in Ashurst Drive in Goring, and he recalls that their detached house had a ten foot high blast wall constructed in the front garden, behind which all the windows of the house were criss-crossed with anti-blast tape; while in the back garden there was an Anderson shelter –

Yes, the Anderson shelter was dug in the garden, [it had] a corrugated iron sort of archway shelter that was put in. You dug in about three feet of ground, put this corrugated arch in, then you put soil on the top of it, and it relied upon that really, just to protect you. Very uncomfortable because they flooded, very damp, catch your death of cold in them and they weren't popular really.

Those with Morrison shelters fared no better. William Guile [b. 1937] remembers how cold the winters were during the 1940s, and that sleeping beneath a large metal shelter made the occupants even colder. All fires had to be put out during a raid – for obvious reasons – so it was very difficult to keep warm. Phyllis Mills [b. 1938] recalls that her mother would take a first aid box and important family documents, such as birth certificates, into the shelter, and during raids she would lie over Phyllis and her sister 'to try and protect us'. Doreen Ayling's [b. 1933] family had been bombed out of London during the Blitz. She remembers coming down to Worthing with her family with all their belongings piled into the back of a removal van. They moved into an old house in High Street, opposite the Swan, and were forced to sell their piano so that room could be made in the small living room for the Morrison Shelter. Doreen remembers that during the day, when her friends came to visit they 'used to use the top of it to practise their tap dancing... it made such a wonderful noise being metal'.

Doreen also remembers the fear she had of air raids, made worse for her by her experiences in London. If the siren sounded while she was at school in nearby Sussex Road, she would try and get home: 'The one thing I do remember, between the houses in Upper High Street there is a passage. If the siren went I would do my utmost to run to that passageway and run home, being so frightened, having been in the Blitz.' Every school had its own shelters, usually dug into the playing fields or built on the playground, close to the school. There would be a ramp leading down to the shelter, and the children were frequently drilled, in the hope that it would become a habit and that there would be no panic if the shelters ever had to be used in the event of a real attack.

Rationing was another feature of wartime life. Introduced at the start of the war, rationing continued for nearly thirteen years. Imported produce, such as bananas, were not available at all while the hostilities lasted. Betty Budd [b.1918], who ran a shop in Worthing with her husband, remembered how the shopkeepers looked after each other, often exchanging items, contrary to the strict rationing rules. For most people queueing was the order of the day. The photograph of the food

Food queues became a common feature of national life, with strict rationing being enforced. These shoppers at Holder's Corner seem happy enough, standing in the spring sunshine, but at other times of the year, queueing was a grim business, especially when the end result may have been little more than a packet of broken biscuits! *Reproduced courtesy Denis Spells.*

queue shows a long, but happy group of potential customers waiting patiently to buy fruit and vegetables from Spells' stall at Holder's Corner. The photographing of such scenes were strictly forbidden, as the government didn't want the outside world, and especially the Germans, to know how difficult it was for the country to feed itself. In the early years of the war there was no rationing in Germany. Alan Wideatt [b.1935] and his family had been evacuated to a little village north of Worthing and coming into town on the 'bus was a treat, although the shopping expedition did not always produce rich rewards –

> *It was a rare occasion for us to go to Worthing on the 'bus but we would go shopping at Potter Baileys, and at that time, they had all the stuff in sacks out on the pavement, and my mum was always very wary of buying anything from outside because the dogs used to come and pee on the sacks. They sold broken biscuits which we always used to buy – we couldn't afford anything else then. That's when you could get broken biscuits.*

Wartime Incidents

Space does not allow for full coverage of all the wartime incidents that took place in Worthing, so this chapter will look at the ones best remembered by our interviewees, which also tend to be the ones that inflicted the greatest damage and loss of life.

On 16th August 1940, a German Heinkel 111P bomber was shot down on the Downs just north of Worthing at High Salvington. This one incident has been the subject of a recent booklet,[8] and has been documented elsewhere (see bibliography). Suffice to say the crashed plane attracted a great deal of interest, with sightseers and souvenir-hunters arriving in large numbers. A number of the crew were killed in the crash, while the survivors were taken prisoner, but not before the novelist and writer Nancy Price, who lived close by, had offered them a cup of tea! Two of our interviewees remembered this incident with different emotions. Alfred Overington [b.1913] was one of the first on the scene –

> *We had a plane came down just north of Cote Street – a German plane. I was part of the First Aid rescue party based in Findon Road at that time. A garage in Findon Road was our headquarters, and we were called out to this plane. Of course we only had the old fashioned sort of car – make-do ambulance – and we went up Cote Street on through the farm there. Unfortunately the German pilot was killed but the plane was there. It wasn't very pleasant.*

Phillip Forrest [b.1921] arrived shortly afterwards with his girlfriend –

> *And there was one aircraft, the Heinkel 111 that came down on Cote Street, by the chalk pit, and Barbara and I cycled up there to have a look at this; and two of the crew were killed and I remember the bodies being taken away in a Corporation truck and they were laid there and you could see the four feet, you know... you were only too pleased to see them go down like that.*

Despite the public being urged to keep ever vigilant eyes open for parachutists only one of our interviewees remembered seeing one come down during the war. Graham Bishop [b.1932] watched as a parachutist came down 'drifting along Goring Road and landed in the back of Trent Road.' This

Left: the immediate aftermath of the German attack in the early hours of 14th September 1940: a familiar street scene strewn with rubble.

Centre: A woman, incongruously wearing what appears to be a fur coat, picks her way through the ruins.

may have been the pilot from a Hurricane, shot down over Goring on the 4th October 1940. As Graham said it was an unusual occurrence – 'the sort of sight you wouldn't expect to see'.

The first major bombing incident in Worthing occurred in the early hours of 14th September 1940, when a total of ten bombs, including an oil bomb, were dropped on the area around the present Town Hall. Despite the severity of the attack, there was only one fatality, although many people had lucky escapes. A sergeant in the Home Guard heard the whistling sound of a bomb, and threw himself to the ground close to the War Memorial and he was soon surrounded by debris from the blast. The front of the Town Hall was dripping oil from the oil bomb attack.

A woman living above a shop on the other side of the road was saved from serious injury or death because she crawled under her bed when she heard the German plane circling overhead. An elderly lady, who had heeded the advice of an ARP warden to sleep downstairs, was very glad she had done so, as the upper storey of her property was destroyed in the blast. Workmen at the Town Hall were just raising the blinds when the raid commenced. At first they thought that the town was being shelled by a German vessel in the Channel, as there seemed to be so many explosions. Parts of the Town Hall and the Assembly Hall were ripped apart by the blasts. One piece of masonry was hurled through the air and crashed into the vestry of Christ Church in Grafton Road.[9] Jacqueline Simpson [b.1930] remembers that the blast wave went down Stoke Abbott Road and shook her house in Christchurch Road, 'leaving a beautiful big crack' in one of the walls.

Stella Sayers [b.1929] was staying with her grandparents in Stanley Road and she recalls that the whole household was shaken by a series of tremendous explosions. As a child of eleven, her greatest concern at the time was for all the animals killed or injured in the pet shop in Chapel Road. Ernie Blackman [b.1929] remembers being told that all the birds were killed but the fish in their tanks survived.

Right: Mitchell's cafe, with its windows shattered and its blind hanging down forlornly, is partially obscured by mounds of debris from neighbouring buildings. *All images reproduced courtesy Worthing Museum.*

Newspaper reports at the time told of a woman who was in bed, cradling her baby, when one of the bombs landed in her garden: she and the baby were blown out of bed and right up to the front door of the house. The woman in question, who must have been sleeping downstairs, was not seriously injured; neither was her baby. She expressed her annoyance that all the seeds she had planted in her garden had been destroyed and a room she had just painted in her house had been ruined. A neighbour was also thrown out of bed by the blast, as he recounted to a reporter –

> *I was in the back room downstairs and the explosion flung me against the wall and knocked me out for a few minutes. I shouted and discovered that my wife and kiddies in the front room were alright. I had a terrible job getting out over all the broken glass and stuff. The door wouldn't open and pieces of the house were falling all the time.* [10]

That afternoon, three bombs were dropped on Pavilion Road. The war had truly arrived in Worthing, yet on this occasion, 13 bombs in total only killed one person.

A raid on the evening of October 8th 1940 left five people dead in Lyndhurst Road and two houses and a shop destroyed. The John Selden pub was seriously damaged. Ernie Blackman [b.1930] had a school friend, George Wheeler, whose parents ran the shop. His friend told him that a man had just come in to buy some cigarettes. He had left and was just getting onto his bike, when the attack started, with the German pilot machine-gunning the street – scattering children playing in the street. The man was not so lucky, and, according to George Wheeler 'had his head shot off.'

George and his sister got under the piano just before the bombs began to fall. They survived the attack and were taken to hospital unwounded, but suffering from shock. Many others were not so lucky, but were killed or maimed in their own homes. Fires soon started to burn and threatened to

The daytime attack on Lyndhurst Road on 8th October 1940 left many dead and injured. The real target was the Gas Works. *Reproduced courtesy Worthing Museum.*

These two views – now and then – show that several properties had to be demolished following the attack: today a car show room occupies the site. *Insert picture reproduced courtesy Worthing Museum.*

pread to a commercial garage in Providence Terrace, from where a fleet of lorries was driven to safety hrough the smoke, firemen, and rescue workers. Onlookers described how an Army sergeant risked is life to search the smoking ruins. He crawled on hands and knees, across shattered roof beams and ast crumbling masonry and fallen ceilings, directing his torch into the gloom, hoping to find urvivors.

The *Worthing Gazette's* reporter described the victims appearing, dazed, from what had been their homes: 'There were pathetic scenes as the people from the evacuated houses scrambled to safety. Most of them were clutching a few treasured belongings in their arms; some were too busy helping the young and the aged to take anything.' The reporter stood back from the scene and recorded that: 'A flock of pigeons, rendered homeless, could be seen circling around the firemen as they stood silhouetted against the fire.'[11]

Bullets from a German aircraft on one occasion pierced one of the gasometers in Lyndhurst Road, with startling results, as Pete Lock [b.1924] recalls: 'All the flames were coming out and it was like a watchman's brazier thing and that's just what it looked like and everybody was rushing up to see this, instead of running away – crowds of people were rushing up there to see what was happening.'

Two high explosive bombs dropped on Haynes Road and Twitten Way, just before 9pm on Saturday 1st November 1941, left seven people dead and 26 seriously injured. Several houses were completely destroyed and many others badly damaged. All the dead were found in the ruins of their homes, although a Mrs Goddard, who was walking home with her husband from a night at the cinema, was also killed by the blast.[12] Half a mile away, another fatality occurred in similar circumstances, as Teri Noice [b.1920] remembers –

The war reaches the suburbs – Haynes Road, 1st November 1941. One man was listening to the radio, singing along to the music when the bombs dropped. *Reproduced courtesy Worthing Museum.*

Left: What hope of finding survivors in this building? Did the bicycles belong to friends and relatives, who had raced to the scene on learning of the attack? *Reproduced courtesy Worthing Museum.*

Opposite: Candia in Lyndhurst Road, the reputedly haunted headquarters of the Home Guard during the Second World War, which contained the local arsenal, including land mines. On the evening of August 9th 1942 it only narrowly missed being hit by a crippled German bomber.

My auntie was walking along Pavilion Road. She got about as far as Jacob's Ladder when it [the bomb] fell. She had her arm... [around]... a friend. And, when the bomb went [off], he got killed. But she was absolutely alright, nothing wrong with her. But he, who she had her arm round, was killed by the blast.

One old soldier, living in Haynes Road, was very lucky to survive, as he explained at the time –

I was listening to the wireless. My wife was in the kitchen and I was in the back sitting room. I did not hear the whistling of the bombs as I was singing to the music. The house seemed to fall in around us. I got to the kitchen as best I could and found my wife with a door and a window on top of her. I got her out somehow. It was a miracle that we both escaped...[13]

One family who had to leave their bombed-out home had only recently moved to Worthing from Portsmouth, where they had been bombed on three separate occasions. They had hoped to find a safe haven in Worthing. Amidst the wreckage, someone put a Union flag up a pole, which seemed to sum up the mood of general defiance.

Arguably the most horrific event of the war in Worthing took place on the evening of the 9th August 1942. Curiously the Air Raid Incidents log records only that one high explosive bomb was dropped in the sea that day and that there were no deaths.[14] Yet, from contemporary newspaper reports and from the eye witness evidence collected for this book, it is clear that there was a calamitous explosion that evening and that at least eight people died.[15] The strange omission from the official record could be due to the incident being neither a bombing nor a machine-gun attack – the two general headings in the log – but the result of a German bomber crashing landing into 'Reydon', the home and surgery of Dr Marjorie Davies on the corner of Lyndhurst and Homefield roads. Of those killed, five were the German crew of the crashed plane; while the other three were Canadian soldiers billeted at Reydon. One can perhaps understand the Germans being excluded from the record, but the Canadians also? Either the omission was an oversight, which seems highly unlikely, or the compilers of the log were restricting themselves to recording civilian deaths. This still does not explain the failure to record the crash landing and the destruction of property which followed. It is an unresolved mystery.

The Heinkel 111 had been hit and severely damaged. Its undercarriage had been shot away and it was leaking fuel. It flew low across Madeira Avenue then crashed through the high flint wall of Candia, the headquarters of the Home Guard, skidded across Lyndhurst Road, leaving behind it a blazing river of aviation fuel, before crashing into Reydon, where it exploded. Several of the Canadian soldiers were covered with burning aviation fuel – at least three of them died, but it is believed others may have died later in Worthing Hospital. Two of the German crew were incinerated, while another was found hanging in a tree. The bodies of the other two were found in the road. Two women in the house – Eva Collins and Carol Wilson – were on the top floor. They ran to the stairs, only to find the staircase engulfed in flames, so they ran to the back bedroom and jumped to safety from the window, before the fire took hold of the upper floor.[16] They were very lucky to survive.

Tug Wilson [b.1927], who was in the Home Guard, remembers that there were deep ruts across

A Heinkel 111 bomber crashed into no.2 Homefield Road and 'Reydon' in Lyndhurst Road, the home of local doctor, Marjorie Davies. Many people, including the crew of the bomber, died at the scene, as a fireball engulfed both properties and burning aviation fuel set the road on fire Amazingly, the damaged properties were not demolished, but rebuilt, as can be seen from these photographs, one taken in 1942, the other in 2011. *Insert reproduced courtesy Worthing Museum.*

Lyndhurst Road, where the plane skidded. It was a terrible incident, but it could have been much worse – Candia contained the Home Guard arsenal, including land mines. If the German bomber had hit Candia the consequences for Worthing would have been terrible and the death toll far higher. Syd Ede [b.1914], who was also based with the Home Guard at Candia, still has vivid memories of that night. He didn't see the crash but remembers that 'the noise was terrific.' He recalls that there were many dead bodies, both in the road and at Dr Davies' house. He also remembers that one of the wheels of the stricken bomber rolled almost to the other end of Lyndhurst Road – a distance of at least half a mile.

On November 10th 1942, 15-year-old Grace Arnold was on her way back home from running an errand to a local shop in Pavilion Road when she was hit by shrapnel from an exploding shell. The subsequent Coroner's Inquest revealed that the death was a result of 'friendly fire' from an anti-aircraft battery. There was a suspicion that the gun crew had not been acting in a responsible manner and the Coroner told Major James Dodd, representing the military, that he wanted an assurance 'that proper and adequate action will be taken in the event of anyone being found negligent.'[17] It is not

Syd Ede, who was serving in the Home Guard at the time, remembered that one of the wheels of the Heinkel rolled to the eastern end of Lyndhurst Road before coming to rest. It was the only substantial remnant of the aircraft that survived, the rest being destroyed on impact on incinerated in the great fire that followed. *Reproduced courtesy Johnston Press.*

known if any disciplinary action did follow. Grace had been found in a state of collapse outside 131 Pavilion Road, where the occupant, Mrs Florence Ware, went to her assistance. Grace had been hit by the shrapnel outside 127 Pavilion Road, where the power of the blast was evident in the destruction to that property, which had all its windows blown in. Dr Rosenberg pronounced her dead at the scene. Grace's sister, Teri Noice [b.1920] had been going to take her younger sibling out for a treat that night –

> She was only 15 and I was very fond of her – we got – although I was older than her – I got on very well with her, and I was going to take her to the pictures that evening and she worked at the bakers, Mrs Hawkins, across the road since she left school. And she came over, she said, 'I can't have any dinner yet, I have to go and get a bottle of milk for Mrs Hawkins, so I said, 'well, don't be long.' And she said, 'I am going to the pictures with you tonight aren't I? I say, 'yes.' Well she was a long time gone I thought; and the Labrador dog we had – she took with her – came back and was all shaking and got underneath the table and I thought, 'whatever is wrong with that dog?' And the next thing was the police came and they said have we got a sister called Gracie, and we said 'yes.' He said 'Well she has just been killed by shrapnel.' And we didn't know anything about it...

Regarding the inquest, Teri remembers that her mother was very upset when one of the officials held up the piece of shrapnel and told Mrs Arnold: 'this is what went in your daughter.' The family felt it was a very insensitive thing to do. They also felt that they were never told the full story of why Grace died.

In the space of three weeks in February and March 1943, Worthing suffered three severe raids, in which 17 people died. Known as 'tip 'n' run' raids, the enemy aircraft would fly low over the Channel, machine-gun the town then drop or 'tip' their bombs before flying back towards France. Although these attacks, which occurred all along the south coast, caused much alarm, loss of life and destruction of property, they were also a sign that Germany was resorting to desperate measures in an effort to sap British morale, as they could no longer organise the large bombing raids on English towns and cities seen earlier in the war.

It was at 2pm on 8th February that four enemy planes descended on the town, travelling from east to west, dropping bombs and machine-gunning as they went. Gladys Ede [b.1921] was working at Chesswood Nurseries, and was making her way up to a café in Ham Road to have some lunch when the raiders struck –

> *... and we were walking up towards the end of Ham Road – end of Lyndhurst Road, going past there and heard this roar and looked up and a plane went directly over the roof tops and he was so low that we could actually see him sitting – him sitting in his plane with his helmet and goggles – he even appeared to be looking down, [we] dived under the wall and then he was gone over, which he had done very quickly. We ran to Ham Road Corner and dived into a doorway and we were immediately thrown out again by the blast from the bomb that he dropped further down the road...*

Dorothy Till [b.1921] who worked with Gladys, remembers that the greenhouses were all shattered by the machine gun bullets from the plane. In the morning they had been picking tomatoes, but in the afternoon they were picking up thousands of shards of broken glass.

The British Restaurant, which was situated in the Labour Hall in Lyndhurst Road, was also hit. Mrs A. Todd, who worked in the restaurant, told a local reporter about her experience: 'We threw

The western side of Homefield Road presents a scene of devestation following the raid of 8th February 1943. Several people, all women, died in this attack. *Reproduced courtesy Worthing Museum.*

ourselves on to the floor and took refuge under tables and anything that was handy. The last customer to leave was a man who sat over there,' she said, gesturing to a scene of splintered timber which had moments before been a table.[18]

Several bombs fell in Homefield Road, where many of the casualties were later found. Mrs F. Goldsmith and her baby had a narrow escape: 'I had just put the baby to sleep in his pram,' she explained, 'He was out of the wind in the conservatory. Then there was a crash and every pane of glass shattered, but, by a miracle, the boy was completely uninjured, although very much scared.'[19]

As the Nazi bombers headed westward they came to St Mary's School by Victoria Park, and here they opened up again with machine gun and cannon. One teacher later described the school being 'cannoned from the front and machine-gunned from the sides,' adding, 'We have never experienced anything like it before and the children, especially the tiny ones, were wonderful. They all gave a remarkable exhibition of self-control.'[20] Another teacher was in an upstairs classroom when the attack began, and also praised the conduct and humour of the children, as she recounted to a local reporter –

I shouted for the girls to lie down just as the first cannon shell smashed a window-frame. The blast hit a blackboard, which knocked me down, while a bullet tore through a second blackboard. Several girls were cut by flying glass, but they all behaved calmly. One of the girl casualties had seen a dentist that morning and had been told she must have some teeth out. She had some nasty cuts on her face; and while we were rendering first-aid she casually remarked, 'well, he won't have to take them out now, the blighter has knocked 'em out.[21]

The Headmaster singled out one of the prefects, Richard Mountain, for particular praise as, on his own initiative, he had carried out the evacuation drill and led the younger children, who were most frightened, to safety in the air raid shelter.

Despite the praise heaped on the children, and the various stories of English resilience and refusal to panic in the face of danger that were a staple of reporting at this time, nothing could disguise the fact that nine people – all women – were killed that day and at least 43 people wounded and injured. The high mortality amongst women can be explained by the timing of the attack – early afternoon – when many women were doing housework and were killed in their own homes.

Only a few days later a parachute bomb dropped on Grove Road at Broadwater, the only bomb of this type known to have been dropped on the town during the war. As it exploded above ground, it caused destruction over a large area. It was sheer good fortune that only two people were killed. Many families were made homeless as several houses were completely destroyed. Some people may have found it ironic that Worthing's former leader of the British Union of Fascists, Captain Budd, had lived in Grove Road. Budd was, of course, at this time in prison, having been interned three years earlier and so missed the chance of being killed or maimed. Roger Davis [b.1929] was living close to the explosion, which he remembers clearly: 'I was staying in the cupboard under the stairs, and there was an almighty bang. The biggest bang of the war, you know. It was a really big, a really big bang. And I was about thirteen at the time... my father was an ARP warden... and I think we were all shocked by the enormity of it. It was really a huge explosion.'

Roger Davis (insert) was a boy of 13 when a parachute bomb fell on Grove Road. He was hiding under the stairs of his home and remembers the huge explosion and the great destruction of property that resulted from the attack. It was the only instance of a parachute bomb (which exploded above ground) hitting Worthing and may explain the large number of military personnel in this photograph, who may have been trying to ascertain what type of device the Germans had used in the raid. *Insert reproduced courtesy Malcolm McCluskey, Worthing Herald; main picture reproduced courtesy Worthing Museum.*

On 9th March, bombs were dropped on Pavilion and St Elmo roads, causing widespread destruction and loss of life. The working men's club was completely demolished, but was rebuilt on its old site after the war. Six people were killed, with three missing, presumed dead. Many were elderly, although one of the fatalities was a four-year-old girl. Coming so soon after the other attacks and deaths, these weeks can be seen as Worthing's blackest of the war. German radio claimed that this particular attack was aimed at 'public utility plants and military installations,'[22] and not civilians. It is doubtful if many people in the town were impressed by that explanation.

Kenneth Wood [b.1938] lived in Pavilion Road at the time and remembers that the road had a disproportionate number of enemy attacks during the war, which he put down to its proximity to the railway line and to Victoria Park, where tanks were stationed for much of the wartime period. He also recalls being told about his father's phlegmatic response to these various dangers –

They bombed the railway line, or tried to bomb the railway line, but they blew up two houses in Pavilion Road and our house was about, what is it, 300, 400 yards [away].... We had broken windows and a big crack in one of our walls appeared outside the house.... We used to hear the dog fights overhead in the aeroplanes. The shells used to splatter on our roof.... I can [tell] a story about my father, who was going to work one lunchtime – he always came home for his lunch and, going back, he was outside pumping up the tyres on his bicycle and then a German plane came – presumably they were firing at the tanks in the park, but they came down across the park and carried on firing down the road, and one of the neighbours said that my father looked up and carried on pumping up his bicycle, got on his bike and rode off to work.

Many of our interviewees remember being forced to dive for cover as enemy planes attacked. Teri Noice [b.1920] was forced to seek cover in a churchyard as she was pushing her baby daughter in her pram. On another occasion she had to throw herself on the pavement as the bullets sped over her, smashing the gate she had just walked past. Phyllis Mills [b.1938] was on a bus travelling along Mill Road when it was attacked. She remembers that the passengers had to run into near by gardens for safety. Ruby Ross [b.1924] also remembers having to run from a bus, this time by Broadwater Church, where she and her friends hid behind the gravestones until the danger had passed. Attacks on buses seem to have been quite common, as many people recall such incidents. Alan Windeatt [b.1935], who had been evacuated to a cottage in a little village north of Worthing, remembered being attacked at home and on a bus –

Pavilion Road was the 'unlucky street' during the war, seeming to suffer more incidents of enemy actions than any other road in Worthing. The picture on the left shows the flattened remains of the West Tarring Working Men's Club, which was rebuilt after the war. *Both pictures reproduced courtesy Worthing Museum.*

No.1 St. Elmo Road reduced to crumpled debris. Incredibly, despite the almost complete destruction of the property, most of the panes of glass in the upper storey window appear to be intact! *Reproduced courtesy Worthing Museum.*

... he came down firing all guns. Our place had a thatched roof and some of those bullets went through the roof and some were incendiary bullets and they set fire to the thatch. I had two experiences of that. Later towards the end of the year, I was on a bus with my mum – a rare trip – we were going to Brighton and we had stopped at the bus stop at the Beeding Cement Works, [where] that row of houses is and we were sitting on the bus and we saw this plane following the river along – thought no more of it – and all of a sudden it opened fire on the bus, but because it had to climb to get up over the hills all the bullets went through the roof and nobody got hurt. Amazing. I was upstairs on the bus with my mother. The bullets went over our heads.

Following the D-Day invasion of France by the Allies in June 1944, it soon became apparent that Germany was heading for defeat. There had been no serious enemy attacks on Worthing for over a year and no fatalities since 14th March 1943. The severe restrictions, including the blackout and the closing off of the beach and promenade, were eased and people started to breathe a little more easily. The Air Raid Incidents log records the last sortie by a German aircraft as taking place on May 30th 1944[23], although after D-Day the recording of incidents appears to have ceased, and does not, therefore, include events that are known to have happened in the town after that date. Richard Norton [b.1924] recalls cycling down to Worthing from London during the summer of 1944, because he had heard that the seafront had been re-opened and he thought it would be a nice day out. However, his excursion almost ended in disaster –

I cycled down from Streatham to the coast. The coast reopened on Saturday night/ Sunday morning, and on Sunday I cycled down. The most significant thing was that I was standing on the front about Heene Terrace, near the Beach Hotel and I saw a plane coming in from the south-west, very low, skimming the sea. At first I thought it was a Spitfire, then from the noise – most of us lads in those days were very keen on aircraft recognition, we knew British, German, American planes – and I knew it wasn't a Spitfire. It was a Messerschmitt 109. It strafed the whole coast, and in those days the [promenade] wall went all the way along, and when he started firing I dodged down behind the wall and on the other side of the wall there were bullets. It all happened in a flash.... Flew in, across the sea, fired, burst of machine gun fire and flew back out to sea, climbing.

In June 1944, the first of the VI or 'doodle bug' flying bombs were seen over Worthing, heading for London. The Press at the time referred to them as 'pilotless planes', and they caused a new panic. Although they were supposed to hit London, they would often run short of fuel before reaching their destination, and crash to the ground in Surrey or Sussex. They were filled with high explosive, so were capable of inflicting damage and casualties. Several VIs passed over Worthing, but only one landed within the Borough boundary, exploding in allotments just behind First Avenue. Several properties were severely damaged, although no one was killed or seriously injured. The attack came on the morning of Saturday 17th June as most people were getting up to have breakfast. One property had the back walls ripped apart, exposing bedrooms covered in hanging plaster from ceilings and rubble on the floors. A neighbour had lost a son in the war: 'This,' she told a reporter, 'is just another job to be faced.'[24]

Ernie Blackman [b.1929] recalled watching a VI flying over Lancing Clump from his parents' bedroom window, the characteristic jet-flame trailing off into the evening sky. Jacqueline Simpson [b.1930] a pupil at Sion Convent at the time remembers that when the droning sound of a VI was heard, the children were ordered under their desks, while the nun crawled under her desk, from where she led the class in reciting a prayer until the danger had passed. Hundreds of VIs, and later the rocket-style V2s, flew over the coast between June 1944 and March 1945, but only the one ever landed on Worthing. This, of course, did not stop the anxiety that one might again fall on the town.

'Holmdale' in First Avenue, badly damaged by the only V.1 or 'doodle bug' bomb to hit Worthing in 1944. These 'pilotless planes' caused great anxiety, and as many passed over the town during the summer of 1944, people were constantly on edge. *Reproduced courtesy Worthing Museum.*

A doodle bug. Had Germany possessed these terrifying weapons earlier in the war, and the even more deadly 'V.2' rockets, they could have seriously weakened the morale of the British public and their resolve to keep fighting the war.

Doreen Ayling [b.1933] has recollections of the happier days of the summer of 1944 being tinged with worry by the ominous sound of the flying bombs –

> *At the time of the doodle bugs, they used to have dances down in Beach House Park. There used to be rose arches on the slightly raised piece [of land], and they used to have music – I'm not sure whether it was played music or a real band, but they used to hold dances there.... out in the open. And the doodle bug would cross there. I was about thirteen I think, at that time, and we went down with friends' parents, and we all dived under this arch, sort of covering our heads. Fortunately, it passed over...*

The last serious incident of World War Two to impact on Worthing took place on 17th December 1944. That day was long remembered in Worthing for what could have happened rather than what actually did happen. A Lancaster Bomber, fully laden with bombs, was en route to Munich, but developed engine problems and was losing power. The plane was heading for a crash landing in Worthing town centre and looked as if it would crash in Montague Street, but at the last minute, the pilot steered the plane away from the hundreds of pedestrians, and onto the beach opposite Heene Road, where the plane exploded. All the crew were killed and three people on the promenade were injured by flying debris, including one man who received a glass splinter in an eye.[25]

The local newspapers received many letters and telephone calls from people who wanted to record their praise for the selfless heroism of the pilot and many of them called for a memorial to be erected in his honour. Surprisingly, it was not until nearly five years later that the identity of the pilot was revealed, when his aunt visited Worthing Town Clerk, Ernest Townsend, to tell him of her nephew's bravery. It transpired that Flying Officer Edward Essenhigh from York and his crew were on their 'Black Gremlin' mission – their thirteenth. It was also revealed that Essenhigh was due to celebrate his 24th birthday the next day and was to be married the next week.[26] Despite the high esteem in which he and his crew were held in Worthing, the only memorial to them is a small plaque on Worthing Pier, which is easily missed by those strolling along the deck, looking out along Worthing's western coastline and over the very spot where the Lancaster came down in 1944.

Notes and References

1   *Worthing Herald*, 4th July 1941

2   *Worthing Gazette*, 16th September 1942, p.5

3   *Worthing Gazette*, 23rd September 1942, p.5

4   *Worthing Herald*, 13th April, 1945, p.7

5   *Worthing Gazette*, 16th September 1942, p.5

6   *World War Two, The Children's View from Mass Observation*, West Sussex History GCSE Project, Unit 3 (West Sussex County Council 1988), p.3

7   See Hare, Chris, *Worthing – a History: riot and respectability in a seaside town* (Philimore 2008), p.183 and Musgrave, Clifford, *Life in Brighton* (Faber and Faber 1981), p.408. The deaths in Brighton were greatly increased by the direct hit sustained by a local cinema, resulting in high casualties. Over 5,000 properties in Brighton sustained bomb damage during the war.

8   Lelliot, *A German Bomber on Worthing Soil*, Graham Lelliott (self-published 2006).

9   *Worthing Gazette*, 18th September 1940, p.5

10 Ibid.

11 *Worthing Gazette*, 9th October 1940, p.5

12 *Worthing Gazette*, 5th November 1941, p.5

13 Ibid.

14 *West Sussex Constabulary Records*, West Sussex Record Office, Pol W/HQ15/5. Although this particular incident appears the most glaring omission, there are other occasions when the record of deaths, for instance, does not tally with those recorded by the local newspapers.

15 *Worthing Gazette*, 12th August 1942, p.5/ *Worthing Herald*, 14th August 1942, front page and p.7

16 *Worthing Herald*, ibid.

16 *Worthing Gazette*, 18th November 1942, back page.

18 *Worthing Gazette*, 10th February 1943, p.5

19 Ibid.

20 *Worthing Herald*, 12th February 1943 (from Robin Baker's Worthing in the Second World War file)

21 *Worthing Gazette*, ibid.

22 *Worthing Herald*, 12th March 1943, front page.

23 *West Sussex Constabulary Records* see note 14, above

24 *Worthing Gazette*, 21st June 1944, p.5

25 *Worthing Gazette*, 22nd December 1944,

26 *Worthing Herald*, 12th August 1949, front page.

10

Afterword:
Post-war Worthing

A new day dawning? In the immediate post-war years, Worthing, like the rest of the country, faced continued rationing and a housing crisis. Most people seemed to want to put the war behind them and build a new future. *Reproduced courtesy Worthing Museum.*

One man's war seemed to sum up the hope and the torment of that long conflict. George Geere [b.1911] was camped with the Royal Engineers at Waterlooville in Hampshire, waiting to embark on the D-Day landings, when, unexpectedly, he got the chance to visit Worthing –

> ... one of my old school pals, name of Perce ['Percy'] Corralls, he was in the same group as me but he was in the Corps of Military Police, and we were under canvas down at Waterlooville and one evening there we were playing cards in the old tents and that, and all of a sudden my old mate looked through the tent flap and he said to me: 'How would you like to get home in the morning, George?' And I looked up and I said, 'Perce, I can't do that.' 'Well,' he said, 'I've got to go down to DHQ [District Headquarters] at Pulborough. I don't know if you'd like to chance it.' Now the Sergeant was in the same tent as me and I looked at him and I said, 'Did you hear that, Jimmy?' He said, 'I heard it. It's up to you. If you get caught, then you know what.' And [we] did, and Perce brought me down on the back of his motorbike – I had to wear a crash helmet in case I got stopped. And Perce said to me, 'I wonder if you'd mind carrying my violin across your knees, George,' because he used to play the violin. He said, 'I shan't need it now.' Well, Perce brought me home, came down to Cowdray Park – a beautiful morning it was – anyhow, I made it and I got back safely. Well, that was it. And then of course on June 6th we landed – poor Perce got killed. Any rate, we've been back to where I landed on two occasions, my son and daughter-in-law take us back and I found Perce's grave, he's buried Caen Cemetery.

George remembered the terrible battles on the Normandy beaches and the heavy fighting that took place as the Allies advanced through France. Yet even amongst the perils of war, George was able to recall special moments of calm and serenity, such as the day they reached the banks of the River Seine –

> And that particular morning, you wouldn't believe it, we was waiting at the side of our boats under our trucks – that's where we slept that night – and it was a beautiful morning, the sun was rising, and looking across the Seine you could see smoke rising from the little old cottages, and I thought to myself, 'now who'd ever think there was a war on?' You could hear gunfire of course, but it was a lovely morning.

George's memories of war, like that of many old soldiers, were a mixture of pride and regret, of

"THEY WON'T PARADE, BUT THEY DON'T FORGET."

[is noted that veterans of the 1939-45 war were absent from Sunday's formal observance of Remembrance Day.]

A cartoon from the *Worthing Herald* in 1946 reflects the fact that few ex-servicemen attended the town's remembrance service that year. The man prefers to dig his allotment and remember fallen comrades on his own, without a military parade or a religious service. *Reproduced courtesy Johnston Press.*

sorrow, but also of hope for a better future. Today, war seems either to be glamorised or turned into a TV spectacular, full of graphs, simulations and politicians, most of whom have never seen military service, explaining the merits of the current conflict. Earl Winterton knew about the reality of war and did not shirk from telling his constituents the truth, even when it was not always what they wanted to hear. It is interesting that after the war, many soldiers wanted to forget and few chose to speak of their experiences. It was reported in 1946 that few ex-servicemen and women attended Worthing's Remembrance Day commemoration at the war memorial, as 'they were fed up with parades.'[1]

Ex-servicemen also objected to Worthing Town Council's plans to build a 'Crystal Garden' in Steyne Gardens as a memorial to those who had died in the 1939–45 conflict. The proposed design consisted of flowers, coloured lights and glass crystal. One unimpressed veteran wondered why they didn't add 'a few Xmas trees as well' to add to the effect.[2] Twelve men signed a letter to the *Worthing Herald* condemning the proposals: 'The whole idea seems designed for the glorification of the town,' they wrote, 'rather than to the memory of the dead.'[3] So great was the feeling of opposition, that the Council abandoned its plans. Eventually it was decided to add the names of the Second World War dead to the existing war memorial by the Town Hall.

Worthing, like most of the country, wanted to forget the war and look to the future. Although there had been much celebration in Worthing on both V.E. (Victory in Europe) Day and V.J. (Victory in Japan) Day in 1945, national plans for an annual Victory Day in June every year did not meet with public enthusiasm. At Worthing a planned carnival was abandoned due to lack of support and later even the planned fireworks were cancelled.[4] People in the town had post-war problems of their own and did not much feel like celebrating. Other old tensions lingered too. Members of the Worthing branch of the Canadian Veterans' Association boycotted the British Legion Remembrance service in 1949, because the organisers would not include the singing of a verse of 'O Canada' in the service.[5]

During 1946 several Worthing women, who had met and fallen in love with Canadian soldiers when they had been stationed in the town, made the long trip across the Atlantic to join them. In March over 800 British women arrived in Halifax, Canada, on board the *Letitia*, including women from Worthing. As they disembarked, a band played 'Here Comes the Bride'.[6] Other Worthing women were not so lucky, and remained in the town to bring up children fathered by Canadian soldiers. Some of these women were married, and their husbands, who had been away fighting in the war, had to cope with the difficult situation of raising children that were not their own.[7]

Although the Home Guard had been 'stood down' in 1944, the women of the Land Army continued in their work for several years after the war. The country was struggling to feed itself, and matters were not helped by the terribly harsh winter of 1947, which despite beginning very mild, ended as one of the coldest on record. Imported goods were scarce, and often included items that children had never seen before, as Phyllis Mills [b.1938] recalls: 'I remember the first time I ever had a banana, because we just didn't know what it was. In fact father got hold of one .... He woke my sister and I up and showed us this banana. Well, even my sister, who is two and a half years older than me, she didn't know what it was either.'

Throughout the winter, the women of the Land Army worked, growing crops and raising livestock. The local Land Army held a demonstration of their work on land near Castle Goring in April 1946, and invited the Press. Tim Walton, who had been a captain during the war, represented the *Worthing Herald*. Walton, perhaps deprived of female company for too long, seemed more interested in the women than their work. His patronising comments appear rather insulting and

Brigadier Otho Prior Palmer, later knighted, was MP for Worthing from 1945-1964. His comparison of the Labour government to the Nazis and his assertion that the Germans would prefer Nazi rule to that of the British, made him a controversial politician.
Reproduced courtesy Johnston Press.

Barbara Wilson of the local Land Army, was subject to some condescending remarks by the reporter from the local newspaper. *Reproduced courtesy Johnston Press.*

ridiculous to a modern reader. 'The Land Girls,' he wrote, 'were all real and pretty enough, even if a little shy.' He did, to be fair, go on to explain that the women had become 'experts in their job,' which included ploughing, harrowing and drilling. Yet his mind was not really on this important work, but on imagining the women in a more sultry setting. That night, he told his readers he dreamt of 'Land Girls ploughing coconut groves in lovely warm sunshine.' The caption to one of the photographs that accompanied Walton's article, which showed a woman driving a tractor, read: 'Attractive Barbara Wilson, pretty young Land Army Cultivation Worker.'[8] Yet, despite such condescension, the country needed women to take on tough jobs. The Territorial Army admitted female recruits for Anti-Aircraft training in 1946, while the Chief Constable of West Sussex, unable to fill vacancies within the Force, advertised for married women – something previously prohibited.

Earl Winterton stepped down as the town's Member of Parliament in June 1945, following the division of the Worthing and Horsham constituency. Winterton continued to represent Horsham for another ten years, while the new Worthing seat was represented by another conservative, Brigadier Otho Prior-Palmer, who continued to serve until 1964. Even before he was elected, Prior-Palmer was ruffling feathers with his uncompromising approach. Within days of the surrender of Nazi Germany, he was alerting the people of Worthing of the dangers of electing a Labour government, 'If we don't watch ourselves,' he warned, 'we will find ourselves in the same position as the Germans in 1933.'[9] He was particularly alarmed by Labour's plans for nationalisation and establishing a National Health Service. Eighteen months later, with Labour in power, his rhetoric became yet more strident. Following a visit to the part of Germany occupied and administered by Britain, he shocked many people by delivering a speech in the House of Commons, during which he alleged that the Germans would rather have the Nazis running their lives than a British socialist government. Prior-Palmer claimed that the Germans were saying, 'If this is democracy, if this is the way a Socialist government runs the country, for God's sake give us Hitler.'[10]

Prior-Palmer's regular tirades against the Labour government are a reminder that politics actually meant something in the 1940s and that real ideological differences separated the parties. For some people, though, the Labour government was not left-wing enough. In the local elections of November 1945, Worthing had its first, and probably only, Communist Party candidate. Jack Sager, who was a fireman in the National Fire Service and had worked for the Co-op before the war, stood in Clifton Ward. Although he came bottom of the poll, he was only 64 votes behind the Labour candidate.[11] Sager's 215 votes in a small ward was quite respectable. It is doubtful if 215 people could be found from the whole of Worthing to vote for a Communist today.

Ernie Blackman [b.1929], at that time a member of the Communist Youth League, remembers Soviet soldiers in Worthing at the end of the war. He used to see them in the amusement arcades, playing on the slot machines. They knew very little English, but would put their fists together and proclaim 'Stalin – he the man', but give a negative gesture for Churchill while declaring, 'nyet!' Many of these Russians may have faced the tender mercies of Stalin's secret police or even have ended up in the Gulag when they returned home, as, in Stalin's eyes, they had been tainted by their association with liberal values and society. Perhaps this was one of the reasons that so many of the Russian soldiers in Worthing drank methylated spirits and even tried to get Ernie and his friends to buy it from them.

The most pressing issue of all in post-war Worthing, as in most of the country, was the lack of affordable housing. Many people were still homeless as a result of enemy action. Young couples, who had put off getting married because of the war, now did so in large numbers, with the result that a great number of births were recorded in these years – the so-called 'baby-boomers', who today are nearing retirement.

A smiling Mrs Bessant trundles her worldly possessions on an old pram to her new home – a disused army hut in Lancing at New Salts Farm. For other homeless families, prefabricated houses, or 'pre-fabs', shipped over from the United States, would be their homes for many years to come. How very different this simple life seems compared to the consumer society we have grown used to today.
Reproduced courtesy Johnston Press.

Many people, desperate for a home, squatted in derelict and empty properties. The novelist Mrs Geraldine Parslowe and her daughter, Mrs Pat England, who had been bombed out of their home in London, squatted in an army hut in woodland near Castle Goring. Mrs Parslowe, with her trademark riding breeches and army beret (which led to her being nicknamed 'Monty', after the famous British general), became something of a cause célèbre. But many hundreds of people were in a similar position and made their homes wherever they could. A Mrs Bessant with her two small children took over former army accommodation near New Salts Farm at Lancing. She was photographed, pushing all her worldly possessions along in an old pram.[12] It was reported that up to 15,000 people in Worthing were waiting for new homes.[13] The Corporation committed itself to building large new Council Estates in Worthing, with the biggest planned for Maybridge. In December 1946, the first prefabricated houses, shipped over from the United States, were erected at Meadow Road in East Worthing.[14] For many families, these temporary structures would be their home for many years to come. It would be more than ten years before the new estates in the town were completed.

Worthing had experienced the difficult years of the Great Depression and had seen heated political debate and confrontation. It then endured six years of war, during which many in the town were visited by death and bereavement. Only slowly did the town and the country recover. By the time the then Prime Minister, Harold Macmillan, told the British public in 1959 that they 'had never had it so good,' he was drawing a line under nearly thirty years of hardship and ushering in the era of consumer goods and individualism, typified by the 'Swinging Sixties'. But that, as they say, is another story.

Notes and References

1   *Worthing Herald*, 15th November 1946, p.11
2   *Worthing Herald*, 15th March 1946, p.9
3   Ibid. p.1
4   *Worthing Herald*, 10th May 1946, p.1, *Worthing Herald*, 17th May 1946, p.1
5   *Worthing Herald*, 4th November 1949, p.1
6   *Worthing Herald*, 15th March, 1946, p.1
7   Hare, Chris, *Through the Hard Times and the Good – an oral and social history of Worthing* (Guild Care 2009), p.113
8   *Worthing Herald*, 26th April 1946, p.1 – 2 and p.20
9   *Worthing Herald*, 11th May 1945, p.9
10 *Worthing Herald*, 29th November 1946, p.20
11 *Worthing Herald*, 5th October 1945, p.1, *Worthing Herald*, 2nd November 1945, p.1
12 *Worthing Herald*, 30th August 1946, p.1
13 *Worthing Herald*, 25th October 1946, p.1
14 *Worthing Herald*, 6th December 1946, p.1 Earlier in the year, the Council had stated that no prefabs would be available during 1946, but the pressure applied by the squatting movement was such that extra resources and officers' time were directed into bringing the re-housing programme forward.

11

Further Reading

Many books have been written on the history of Worthing, but the following are books that concentrate on the 1930s and 40s. They appear alphabetically by author.

Worthing Books

An Anthology of the Worthing Tramocars (Southdown Enthusiasts' Club 2002)

Clark, Colin and Taylor, Rupert, *Worthing at War* (Beckett Features 1989)

Hare, Chris, *Through the Hard Times and the Good – an oral and social history of Worthing* (Guild Care 2009)

Holden, Paul, edited by, *Worthing at War – the diary of C.F. Harriss* (Phillimore 2010)

Lelliott, Graham, *A German Bomber on Worthing Soil* (self-published 2006)

Payne, Michael, *Storm Tide – Worthing: Prelude to War 1933–1939* (Verite CM Ltd 2008)

Strange, Joan, *Dispatches from the Home Front, the war diaries of Joan Strange 1939–1945* (Monarch 1989)

Regional Books

Crook, Paul, *Sussex Home Guard* (Middleton Press 1998)

Goodman, John, *Defending Sussex Beaches* (Middleton Press 2010)

Hylton, Stuart, *Battlefield Britain – Kent and Sussex 1940 – Britain's Front Line* (Pen & Sword 2004)

National Books

Gardiner, Juliet, *The Thirties: An Intimate History* (Harper Collins 2009)

Gardiner, Juliet, *Wartime: Britain 1939–45* (Headline 2004)

Waller, Maureen, *London 1945* (John Murray 2004)

Index

Index of interviewees
with birthdates and captions